40 Ways to Raise a Nonracist Child

40 Ways to Raise a Nonracist Child

Barbara Mathias
Mary Ann French

HarperPerennial
A Division of HarperCollins*Publishers*

HarperCollins books may be purchased for educational, business, or sales promotional use. For information, please write to: Special Markets Department, HarperCollins Publishers, Inc., 10 East 53rd Street, New York, New York 10022.

FIRST EDITION

Library of Congress Cataloging-in-Publication Data

Mathias, Barbara, 1940–
    40 ways to raise a nonracist child / Barbara Mathias, Mary Ann French. — 1st ed.
        p.   cm.
    ISBN 0–06–273322–2
    1. Prejudices in children—United States—Prevention. 2. Racism—United States—Prevention. 3. Race awareness in children—United States. 4. Child rearing—United States. I. French, Mary Ann. II. Title.
BF723.P75M36 1996
649'.7—dc20   96-7389

98 99 00 ❖/RRD 10 9 8 7 6 5

To my children, Lisa, Janet, Matthew, Lindsey and John

Barbara Mathias

For French Scott Marshall—may the ancestors
always guide him well
And for Carolyn H. and David M. French—
in humble hindsight of their prodigious parenting

Mary Ann French

Contents

Acknowledgments

We couldn't have written this book without the help of hundreds of parents who shared their experiences, their hopes, their fears and their wisdom. We are also indebted to the many school principals who gave us their support and encouraged us to meet with their students and faculties.

We are grateful to the following people for their professional guidance: Mary Stewart Bargar, Joy Baxt, Lisa Blair, B.J. Childress, Fred Cooke, Judy David, Kevin P. Dwyer, David Elkind, Martha Hansen, Melissa Helmbrecht, Mary Henry, Sister Monica, Chris Moore, Lester Olinger, Layli Phillips, Judy Press, Penrose Ramsey, Ed Repa, Carrie Rivers, Jacqueline Samuel, De Vora Slavin, Laurence Steinberg, Sophia Wong and Chip Wood.

For their powerful insights—whether experiential, theoretical or both—we thank Diane and Wayne Bowman, Sharon Thornburgh Brown, Jill H. Bullitt, Carolyn Cobden, Margaret DeLorme, Louise Derman-Sparks, Edwin Dugas, Carolyn Howard French, Joseph B. French, Beverly Gray, Janice E. Hale, Vivian R. Johnson, David Levering Lewis, Darci Glassman Lieb, Peggy McIntosh, Jane and Gus Martin, Marilyn Milloy and Joseph Windham.

Special thanks to Ruth Holder, for her extraordinary ocular, auditory and advisory capacities. The same to Deborah Heard and David Von Drehle for their abundant patience, confidence and goodwill. Thanks to Dorothy M. French for being herself.

Our agent, Chris Tomasino, and our editor, Rob Kaplan, have believed in this project from the start, and for that we are blessed and grateful.

Introduction

Barbara Mathias

There is a certain risk in presenting the topic of racism in such a brief format as "40 Ways"—the danger being that the book may be judged as minimizing the seriousness and the complexity of the topic. Nothing could be further from our intentions. Our choice of format grew out of our intent to be practical and realistic. Through personal experience we know that today's parents have little time or patience for reading more theory on child raising; and yet, they have little clear guidance on one of the most crucial aspects of parenting—how to respond to the racism that permeates their children's world. (It was disturbing to find that the majority of parenting books don't cover or even mention racism, as if it weren't a major factor affecting child development.) Parents need to know what to say when their three-year-old wants to be "another color" like one of his friends in nursery school, or when their fifteen-year-old is terrified of the racial tension in her school. They also need to educate themselves on how prejudice impacts a child's particular developmental stage from early childhood through adolescence. For instance, why an eight-year-old is so generous and fair in his friendships, only to become more socially judgmental when he reaches prepuberty.

This book has six sections: The first addresses all parents of children of any age; the remainder cover the five developmental stages of childhood and how they are affected by racism. Throughout the book we describe the racism that exists in the home, in school and throughout the community. We also touch upon the special needs of immigrants, international adoptions and mixed-race families. We ask all parents to identify the prejudice that goes back for generations in their families. We discuss the tendency students have to congregate by race, as well as the sham of poorly planned academic programs that masquerade as multicultural education. We make clear why it is so hard to make adult interracial relationships work, a prerequisite for being role models for our children. Most important, and intrinsic to each of these forty ways, we ask parents to face up to and talk about racism with their children and other adults.

This discussion is not just about blacks and whites, though that is often our focus because of the pattern of discrimination that has long been dominant in our American society. Here we speak to all parents—Asian, Hispanic, Native American—and all the cultural variations within and between those races. Our sources of information come from educators and experts on child development, as well as from the anonymous testimony of parents and children throughout the country. We are particularly grateful to these families for their honesty and willingness to participate in this important project.

Halfway through the process of writing this book Mary Ann and I realized that our collaboration was a microcosm for what we were asking parents to do—interact with and accept people of other races. Mary Ann is black; I am white. With no history of friendship to boost us, we came together as journalists interested in writing a book on how racism affects children and their future. It all started out very polite and professional with just a touch of the uncertainty that comes with any collaboration. However, as we delved deeper into the project and our different perspectives became more obvious, it seemed we couldn't escape the clashes and pain. There were times when we argued vehemently, and one particular "lost weekend," we insulted and questioned each other's views with a passion that threatened to end our project. Despite and because of all this, we have become friends, and our dialogue on race continues—as I imagine it will for years to come.

How did we work through our differences? By considering and discussing several contributing factors. First, as a white person, I could intellectualize the pain of minority peoples, but I couldn't experience it or describe it to the degree that Mary Ann did in her faxes to me or during our conversations. I had an extremely difficult time detecting and admitting to the racist nuances Mary Ann kept pointing out to me. Certainly, I was aware of prejudice in the world, but I didn't see it in every corner. Now I had to sensitize myself to the inequities in life. In time, I couldn't read a magazine or watch television without being aware of how few minorities were represented or how they were stereotyped. I couldn't go to a party or event without counting the numbers of whites versus minorities. I couldn't converse with my black and Asian friends without wondering if I felt superior. While interviewing grade school and high school children from other races, I was often brought to tears as they openly expressed their frustrations with our culture of white supremacy. And when interviewing parents from other races, I often wanted to walk away and get back to the comfort and privileges of my white world. I felt ashamed, but I would tell myself that their sufferings were too big and too unwieldy for me to handle.

Second, Mary Ann and I had dramatically different ways

of expressing ourselves. The temptation for me was to label Mary Ann as the "angry black," and I'm sure she could have tagged me as the "indifferent white." But our task was to break down stereotypes, not perpetuate them. After the dust settled, I told her that I have always been nonconfrontational because it worked best with my parents and siblings; and she told me that she has always been outspoken just like her parents and many of her siblings. Furthermore, she knows whites who, like her, are confrontational, and likewise, I know blacks who are nonconfrontational. The source of our differences was as much our inherent personalities and our histories of family dynamics as it was race.

Third, there is a difference in our ages and our stages of motherhood. I am in my fifties, recently divorced and the mother of five grown children. Mary Ann is in her forties and the recently divorced mother of a six-year-old son. Though not a generation apart, our experiences are worlds apart. When the feminist revolution and the debate over Vietnam were raging, I was diapering three small children and caught up in keeping the family running. I never had the involvement in social issues that Mary Ann and many of the women her age did. Until my youngest child was born, I was fortunate not to have to work outside the home; but once I started working, I was drawn to writing on family and women's issues. It is only in the past 15 years that I have learned to question and challenge the unfairness inflicted on minorities and women. Mary Ann has been in the thick of this debate from the time she was a young child.

This is what we all need to do when we relate to people from other races. As you become impatient or annoyed with the way you see things differently, you must consider all the factors at play that make you who you are, and the other person who she is. You both need to talk about and recognize the influence of your culture, personality, age, money, education and family circumstance—for example, the fact that your grandmother raised you or that you never traveled beyond your hometown until your adult years.

From the start of this project I let Mary Ann know that I was writing this book more out of regret than out of experience. Yes, I raised five children, all of whom attended public schools with racially diverse populations. And from the time they were very little, I taught my children to respect others, just as they should respect one another. But as for discussing racism or prejudice specifically, those words came up only if the children initiated it, which was rarely. Like many white parents during the '70s and up through the early '90s, I was able to skirt the issues surrounding racism and somehow keep a clear conscience. Fortunately, perhaps miraculously, my children are not racist. But there are still issues to talk about—such as the racism on their college campuses or in their workplaces. Through the work on this book, I am learning how to bring up the topic of racism with them, express my opinions and listen to theirs. It's never too late to parent against prejudice. If and when my children marry and have children of their own, I plan to be a very forthright grandmother, full of questions and challenges for my grandchildren.

Last May I met with a group of immigrant students—all seniors—at Einstein High School in Kensington, Maryland. After a very lively discussion, one of the boys from Nicaragua stayed behind to talk more. "Discrimination is bad. . . . This book is good; what you are doing is good," he said, in a warm and congratulatory tone. Then more passionately, he added: "I want someday to be a good father. I want my boy to know these things."

It is with that same passion and hope for the future that Mary Ann and I have dedicated ourselves and our work to help parents raise their children to respect all people. Both of us are convinced that in order for the races to survive together in a fair and productive society, we have got to learn to talk and accept our differences. Indeed, we may even enjoy and thrive on our differences.

Introduction

Mary Ann French

The first time we talked seriously about doing this book, I asked Barbara what she thought it would take—short of a miracle—for white people to truly care about racism and its poisonous effects. For people of color, of course, the motive is clear. Our interests are totally invested. But what would it take for white people to face up to racism, as most minorities do every day? I posed the question both rhetorically and hopefully, in the dual Du Boisian sense that African Americans know so well. In other words, just as surely as I would not hold my breath waiting for some(white)one to answer the question, I knew I must continue to ask it, to search for some kind of solution, lest something die inside of me. Such is life for the African in America.

Which is not to say that we are without blame in this mess. I was forced to focus on my own creeping complicity late one recent sleepless night while channel-surfing. I caught a rerun of Eleanor Holmes Norton—the District of Columbia's Delegate to Congress—speaking to a crowd of constituents during a Martin Luther King Day celebration. The longtime civil and human rights activist was fussing at her people and calling them to account as few others can. She reminded us that King's power came from his heart and from the purity of his pleadings. That just as he demanded equal, respectful treatment, he was willing to proffer it. She pointed to places where some black people have been backsliding and losing their moral high ground—deflecting their own miseries by disdaining Jews or women or homosexuals. She reminded us that our most abiding source of strength throughout our many travails in this "new" world has been our souls. She scolded us lovingly, however, and acknowledged the logic in our despair.

Too many of us never properly grieved the death of the dream. When the times changed and the economy crashed, we turned tough instead, whether we were in the streets or in boardrooms. The self-centeredness of the '80s wasn't so completely new; the '70s had its moments, too, when many of us plunged right into that mainstream and strapped on someone else's values for safety as we tried to stay afloat.

And what has it gotten us? Aside from an ever-deepening need to even the score. Justice doesn't always call for vengeance, however sweet or justifiable it might be. Paybacks end up costing everybody involved, I reason selfishly. Plus, I want more than a reactive life for my son.

"I have one great fear in my heart," the South African writer Alan Paton had one of his black countrymen say in the novel *Cry, the Beloved Country,* "that one day when they turn to loving they will find we are turned to hating." It's hard. Our sorrows entitle us to a whole lot of bitterness. There's no denying that. But is it worth collecting? The challenge would seem to be, as it always has been, to rise above and soar beyond. To not be sullied.

My dear departed grandmother—Dorothy Waring Howard—founded one of the nation's first preschools, and she did it in the segregation of Washington, D.C. She had students of many colors and nationalities, although they were

predominantly African American. Several generations of grad-
uates from her Garden of Children testify still to the invalu-
able grounding she gave them for life—socially, emotionally,
physically and cognitively. Her secret? She refused to
acknowledge racism. She snubbed it. She saw it as absurd and
nonsensical, beneath her contempt. She wouldn't honor it
with her attention.

Admittedly, that approach was more practical in the
cocooned world of segregation. Now there's no way not to
notice racism. It's all up in our faces, every day. So maybe it's
time for new tactics. But the goal should remain the same, says
my mother, Carolyn Howard French, an early-childhood development specialist who taught in my grandmother's school
before founding a preschool herself—Crispus Attucks, in
Roxbury. "How do you best raise a child in a racist world?" she
asks, echoing my question. "The simplest answer is the oldest
answer: Make sure the child has a parent's love and a healthy
self-image."

It's simple—but far from easy or painless. As we
launched our research for *40 Ways to Raise a Nonracist Child*, I
halfway hoped that we'd find some overlooked or forgotten
antidote to racism. Or even better, a vaccine. A solution that
at worst would require periodic boosters. But, alas, there are
no magic tricks. What we found were many small and sensible steps which when added together, seem to have the mak-
ings of miracles.

As long as there are children, there is hope. Each generation brings with it another chance to restore balance and grace
to our world. Let's try to raise our children without twisting
their minds with adult fears and falsehoods. We have a long
way to go; here is where we start.

My mother was one of the first people I talked to after
deciding to work on this book—both because of her expertise

in the field of early-childhood development and because I often turn to her when launching a new project—or to my dad or one or several of my seven siblings. I'm sure I'll be consulting my son more as he matures, too. For we are all one. Family. However widespread, we share that base. And it's not just about a gene pool.

A family stands or falls on its values: beliefs and behaviors that are honed over lifetimes and then passed on, simply strengthened or wisely revised. Inherited habits are heritage, as customs are culture. Many such families make a people.

When I was a kid there always seemed to be someone hanging around our house simply wanting to be in the exuberence of our midst. We were entertaining—a bit wild, sometimes foolish, often witty and most times curious. We amused ourselves by taking as many detours as possible without losing our way. We were our own little culture. Despite all of our individual differences, we saw life from similar vantage points and shared pretty much the same world view. As we matured and moved on, we naturally referred to that world view to form our principles—which, as you might expect, are not all about staid standards of behavior. I think it's fair to say we insist on a certain amount of humor, some depth if there is to be debate, sarcasm when called for and so on.

Families are different now, and values no longer can be grafted onto children so gradually, so naturally. There isn't time. Marriages don't last 50 years, as my parents' has to date. Half of them end in divorce, as both Barbara's and mine did while we were working on this book. We didn't undergo the full trauma while writing, mind you. It was more a matter of the paperwork catching up to the reality of our lives. At any rate, as divorced parents experiment with new family formulations and struggle to instill values in their children, we believe there will be more nonracist children in the making.

For we shall have to be more tolerant. The days of cultural and family insularity are all but over. Why not take an active hand in determining what comes next?

Barbara says that during our collaboration, she was tempted to label me an "angry black." I have always chafed at that characterization of anybody black, if only for the reason that we've got plenty to be angry about. The label effectively discounts the validity of our feelings and our experiences, stressing instead superficialities such as our demeanor and decorum. Thus I was particularly gratified while working on this book to come across white people who also are passionate in their opposition to our country's racism. Peggy McIntosh, the Associate Director of Wellesley College's Center for Research on Women, is an example. Check out what she has found, taken here from her paper on "White Privilege and Male Privilege": "As a white person, I was taught to see racism only in individual acts of meanness, not in invisible systems conferring dominance on my racial group. I think whites are carefully taught not to recognize white privilege, as males are taught not to recognize male privilege. I have come to see white privilege as an invisible package of unearned assets which I can count on cashing in each day, but about which I was meant to remain oblivious. White privilege is like an invisible, weightless knapsack of special provisions, maps, passports, codebooks, visas, clothes, tools and blank checks. . . .[W]hites are taught to think of their lives as morally neutral, normative, average and also ideal, so that when we work to benefit others, this is seen as work which will allow 'them' to be more like 'us.'. . . The pressure to avoid seeing [white privilege] is great, for in facing it I must give up the myth of meritocracy. . . the myth that democratic choice is equally available to all. Keeping most people unaware that freedom of confident action is there for just a small number of people props up those in power and serves to keep power in the hands of the same groups that have most of it already." After listing 46 "unearned privileges" that America automatically grants her, but rarely affords the African American women alongside whom she works, McIntosh writes: "If these things are true, this is not such a free country; one's life is not what one makes it; many doors open for certain people through no virtue of their own."

Barbara and I fervently hope that our children will have a more even shot at life. It's time to be free of this foolishness. We implore you to join us as we set new sights.

Advice for All Parents

1

Raise Your Replacements with Principle

Perhaps it's obvious—as much of the advice on these pages may seem at first glance—that our mission as parents is to prepare our children to take our places in this world.

But somehow it's easy to forget that they soon will be our peers—let alone our survivors.

We have a mammoth ability to shape them now. Tomorrow, they will be our equals in both size and strength, which they will use in ways that are brute or kind, according to how we have raised them. What will they see through the lens we provide? What kind of America will they dream at the end of our day?

Some of the most thoughtful and effective parents we interviewed for this book are not exceedingly religious but talk in nearly sacred terms about their approach to parenting. They are deeply committed to guiding principles that vary in emphasis but that all could be considered "golden rules." Their goals are both simple and all-consuming. They aim to raise up children who are fit for society. At the same time, they strive to make that society more fit for all. They begin by devising guidelines, within which they then endeavor to live. Sound easy? Self-evident?

Deborah, a Cincinnati mother of three girls—ages two, five and seven—and her husband decided early on to concentrate on teaching their children to respect all races equally. The family—which is Jewish—has lost immediate relatives to Hitler's concentration camps, forbears to a Russian czar's pogrom, as well as ancestors to slavery in Pharaoh's Egypt.

"I try to use every opportunity that comes along to teach my children to treat other people as they would like to be treated," Deborah says. "I tell them, 'Remember, you were once slaves'—the line from Passover—and 'Remember Hitler. Remember that you never want anything like that to happen to anybody else in this world.' "

It's tough, though. Deborah says her children were confused recently as they watched her nearly destroy a friendship with Janet, another mother in their middle-class neighborhood, who is black. The damage was done during a discussion the two women had about Nation of Islam Minister Louis Farrakhan and the historic Million Man March he organized in Washington, D.C. Deborah wanted Janet to denounce and disavow Farrakhan, whom many believe to be anti-Semitic.

Janet, however, needed Deborah to understand that Farrakhan was not her focus. Instead, she was thrilled by the sight of hundreds of thousands of African American men converging in the nation's capital to pledge a stronger commitment to themselves and to their families.

After leaving Janet's house in a huff, Deborah tried to explain to her children—who were more accustomed to their mother preaching tolerance than excommunicating friends—

how and why some of her principles supersede all others. It wasn't easy. Deborah now doubts whether she was completely fair with Janet and isn't sure she ever made her reasoning clear to her girls. She does know, however, that she acted and spoke from her heart. She also misses her friend and is searching for a way to bridge the gap with Janet without feeling she's betraying her people—a move she says will please her daughters no end.

Deborah's children may be too young now to understand the intricate ways in which their mother's beliefs overlap and sometimes conflict, but she is teaching them a larger lesson by acting honestly and not hiding the hurt that sometimes results. In fact, Deborah may already have taught them enough to accept—even when she can't—that life is messy, and that loyalties can compete without necessarily nullifying principle.

We Americans often struggle when it comes to selecting and sticking to a philosophy of child rearing. We're not known for the strength of our planning. By and large, we're not into saving either. When the inevitable rainy day comes, we tend to count more on our knack for spur-of-the-moment solutions. That has been the source of many of our nation's triumphs as well as its downfalls.

We delight in our flexibility. We are undaunted as we attempt to juggle an impossible number of demands. We fumble regularly, and things of substance slip our grip. Then we vow to take up the challenge anew the next day. And we believe everything will work out. Somehow.

Many of the ways we offer here to help raise your child righteously in our racist world are rooted in systems of beliefs and convictions. Such strategies for living life fairly come in many forms, both sacred and secular, but most of them have similarly humane foundations. Adopt one, follow it, and you're likely to find yourself stumbling less as a parent. You may still lose your way occasionally, but you'll have a compass to get back on course. And getting back to the obvious, it will be easier to guide and inspire your children to follow you if you're true to your principles.

2

Why White Parents Should Care

When the idea for this book was in its formative stage, Barbara wondered: What it would take for white people to truly care about racism and its negative effects on people. Most of the whites she interviewed believe in a sense of decency and fairness for all human beings. Unfortunately, she knew that for herself, and for most other whites, when it comes to dealing with racism, we have a short memory and an even shorter attention span—we grow impatient, tiring of all the complaints, accusations and cries of victimization from minorities, and we just want the problem to go away. We want to get on with our lives.

Before we can serve as models for our children, whites need to examine why we have such a hard time sustaining our interest and motivation to end racism. Where does our apathy come from?

To begin, consider how often you are reminded of your race. When you look in the mirror? Not really. You're probably more interested in whether you look clean, appear attractive or have nice teeth. Probably the only time you really think about being white is when you're the only one in a room full of minorities—and that happens rarely or never. Even when you're in the company of one or two minorities, waiting for a bus or in a meeting at work, you think of the minority's race more than of your own.

Now put yourself in the minority person's shoes. Imagine being reminded of your race every time you look in the mirror, walk down the street, go into your office, walk into a store, attend a ball game, go to a movie or a restaurant—every time you step outside your home, knowing and feeling that you are being silently singled out and judged by the color of your skin. Or that every time you read a magazine, watch television or go to the theater, you are reminded that your race is either unfairly represented, or not represented at all.

Some of our apathy as whites, then, is because race is not a daily issue for us, as it is for the minority. And we prefer to deny that we participate in making it an issue for the minority.

"Why do blacks make everything the whites' problem?" a white woman named Beth argues with Alice, a black friend from her office. "Because whites are responsible for this mess!" exclaims Alice, barely able to contain herself. Beth is equally upset. "We didn't do this; it was our ancestors. Don't lay all this guilt on us."

It's true that our white ancestors initiated the crimes of racism, and most of us now think we are innocent of any outward acts of oppression towards minorities; but we need to acknowledge our private power struggle with minorities. Our unspoken belief is, "We whites are better people than you." That is called racism. And whether we like it or not, we reflect that thinking in how we treat other races. This is what the minority knows when a cop pulls him over just because he is driving an expensive car; this is what a minority feels when he gets in an elevator with a white person who nervously chats with him about everything under the sun or keeps looking the other way. Minorities feel and know our fear of them and our power over them.

Now consider how things are changing because of such influential events and issues as the O. J. Simpson verdict, the battle against affirmative action and possible congressional cutbacks of government programs: It seems as though minorities—particularly blacks—are constantly complaining about racism. Suddenly they are making racism our problem every waking minute. As the pressure and anger continue to mount, most whites can't stand the heat. We have little choice but to yield—and to work together in this process. The alternative is too frightening and dishonorable even to consider. For if whites ignore racism and continue to feed it and allow it to grow, we leave to our children an increasingly violent and shameful world. Unless we open up communications between the races we will be handing the next generation all the social ills that come with our polarization. We owe a better life to all children. That alone should be motivation for white parents to overcome their apathy to racism.

3

Examine Your Reluctance to Form Interracial Friendships

If you are to be a role model for your children, you need to make an effort to broaden your world: You need to get to know people from other races. Before we suggest positive ways to meet and communicate with others, it is important for you to examine the reasons why most adults find such interracial relationships difficult to establish, and often impossible to maintain.

In most friendships—even casual relationships—we are drawn to people like ourselves because it gives us a sense of parity, safety and pleasure.

What we assume through prejudice or ignorance is that people of other races are *totally* different from ourselves, not only in how they look or in the foods they eat or in the music they like but also in the ways they raise their families or in their most fundamental beliefs and hopes.

We find it difficult to recognize that we are all human beings who feel the same range of emotions. We realize, rationally, that we can enrich our lives by learning about other peoples and exploring our cultural differences. But we tend to dismiss that fact. Many people, when taking a shot at interracial friendship, find it so disquieting and awkward that they tiptoe around each other for fear of embarrassing themselves, or being rejected or some other equally dire unknown. This holds for both minorities and whites.

Many others, unfortunately, refuse to even try socializing across the color line—often out of deep anger or simply a stubborn unwillingness to change. One black high school student who has given workshops on diversity for parents of all races observes: "Parents seem very indignant about what grieves them in their lives. They are very defensive about prejudice. They are very bitter about the past."

There is also the matter of blacks and whites constantly measuring the extent of the other's commitment to social integration. They sometimes accuse the other—though rarely openly—of not putting in equal time and effort to get acquainted. And if others don't, why should they? Some white women complained to Barbara that they invited black women to their homes, but the invitation was never returned. "I'm always the one to make the effort," a white mother said, testily. "They not only don't invite me back, they don't even invite my son." Mary Ann says that she's heard similar complaints from black mothers, many times. Some blacks say that the whites' invitations seem "insincere" in that they are just invited for race-related events or some do-gooder party where the whites earn "points" for a black being present; they complain that they are never invited for their individual selves but as a representative of their race.

Some whites were concerned that their efforts at interracial friendship would appear to be "contrived." A white woman from suburban Ohio says: "I worry about taking on a friendship with a minority as if it's a project; it seems very condescending to me." It *is* condescending as long as she thinks that the person is not her equal, or if she considers that person's life so different from hers that it seems foreign or threatening.

This reluctance to bridge the racial gap socially isn't limited to blacks and whites. Hispanic and Asian parents who were interviewed also expressed a strong preference to socialize with their own groups, though they seemed well aware of how such closed circles kept them from being understood by others and perpetuated polarization and racism.

Once you consider all these reasons for not wanting to forge interracial relationships—and understand that most of them are based on the fear of rejection and the power of racial prejudice—you are ready to move on to the next way.

4

Make Acquaintances Across Color Lines

We don't expect you to make a friend every time you bump into a person of another race. We realize that is unrealistic. However, we are saying that if you are tired and ashamed of racism, or fed up with how it is affecting your family and society, you should get to know other people from other races. After all, your example will speak volumes to your children.

The only way to rid yourself of the prejudices you've so long held is to know the other person intimately. When you make an effort to connect with several people from another race, and you come to respect them, you are more likely to feel an empathic connection towards their race as a whole.

How do you do it?

Go beyond the perfunctory, polite greetings in the workplace; ask the "other" person to meet for a cup of coffee or have lunch. If they turn you down, they may be genuinely busy, so don't be insulted, try again later.

When you spend time together, you don't have to have an in-depth discourse on racial differences; just talk about your family, your interests, your car, your dog, the movie you saw last weekend, the book you're reading, whatever is bugging or pleasing you at home and at work. Expect to say the wrong thing once in a while, or even frequently. Speak up when you feel misunderstood during the discourse. Eventually, we all have to learn to say, "Hey, you just made an assumption about me that doesn't fit." If you do want to talk about race and cultural differences, agree that honesty is acceptable, no matter how painful.

Don't think that one conversation is going to make you buddies or instantly enlighten you about the other's race. It takes lots of conversations, good and bad; what's important is your sincerity and interest.

Don't expect all or any of your interracial relationships to be close. Just like the relationships you have with your own people in your own group, there are varying degrees of friendship. Closeness can't be forced; it comes with shared needs or interests. Aim for understanding, respect and kindness, no matter what the depth of the relationship.

A white woman from the Southwest describes her close friendship with a black woman from New York as "very close now that we've gotten past that race thing." Some would argue that race is always pertinent to the interracial friendship: "Don't ever forget that I'm black," said one woman to her white friend, "because I don't." Whichever way you want it, it's important to agree on the role of race in a relationship.

Just as you have to be patient with your children's interracial skills, be patient with your own—it takes courage, practice and bruised egos. Mary Ann and Barbara started this project as virtual strangers, two people who only nodded in the hallways at *The Washington Post* and then suddenly came together with the idea of this book and a deep concern for their children's future. There was no instant closeness or comfort in their collaboration. They spent months doing the racial tiptoe dance, trying not to say things that insulted each other (still managing to many times, as they wrongly assumed what the other was thinking and feeling). When they finally opened up, it was "brutal," as Mary Ann would say, and yet, they both agree that their painful beginnings were worth it. They became sensitive to each other's concerns and respectful of each other's views. In that process, they not only gained in friendship but also in the experience of each other's race.

5

Trace Your Family's History of Prejudice

No family's history is void of prejudice or the pain of racism. Perhaps your parents and their parents before them held strong views about race, class, religion, politics and lifestyles, but they were rarely expressed openly. Nevertheless, those views made their impression and became such a part of your present-day thinking that you probably have forgotten their origins. If you want to understand why it is you feel the way you do about people unlike yourself, you need to do some sleuthing about your family background. This very personal process will help you in several ways: It will define your present point of view; help you rethink your opinions on race and racism; and enable you to communicate better with your child by breaking family patterns that are destructive or misleading.

Some parents may choose to do this investigation along with their child. But if that would make you feel uncomfortable, do it on your own first. You may decide to discuss your family history with a small group of parents who are friends, or members of a school organization. Whichever way you do it, privately or with your child or publicly with other parents, remember that this isn't going to be a fun exercise or something that is taken lightly. Uncovering the injustices that have been in your family for generations can be painful, whether you have been the victims or the perpetrators.

Ask the following questions: When were you first aware of people unlike yourself, in race or way of life? Note whether you were very young (under the age of six) or whether it was much later (in your teens); the answer can help you evaluate your degree of exposure to racial issues. Barbara found that white people's recognition of racial distinctions often didn't begin until the middle-school years, while minorities were aware of whites from early childhood, usually because their parents spoke to them about race, and because they vividly recalled being treated differently by white people.

What were your feelings about those unlike yourself? Be honest, even if the memory is uncomfortable.

Can you recall how your parents expressed their feelings about other races? Did your grandparents' view have a strong influence as well? Did those opinions of your parents and grandparents coincide or conflict? Often, we heard that the older generations—both black and white—"ignored" the issues or "refused to dignify the problem" with their attention. Given what we know about the history of this country, it is likely that such a neutral stance or denial was a defense mechanism against circumstances beyond their control.

Was race talked about openly in your family, or was it mentioned only in off-hand remarks, jokes and stereotypes?

Did you determine how your parents felt about race not by what they said but by how they lived and how they treated others?

Were there heated arguments? Were threats made, such as if you dated someone from another race or religion, you would be punished—or even disowned?

When and how did you realize that there was prejudice in your family? Usually, the memory comes back with a particularly poignant or dramatic event. A woman who grew up in a comfortable, white neighborhood always believed that her parents were "liberal thinkers." It wasn't until the first black family moved in and her family was the first to move out that she realized how her parents really felt.

Examine the external factors that influenced your family's opinions about race. How diverse was your neighborhood, school, church or synagogue? How did your teachers and friends feel about other races? What were the racial issues in the country and in your community during your upbringing? Was it a time of open discrimination or "tolerance"?

Finally, ask yourself how your parents' beliefs influenced your behavior outside of the family. For example, when there were race issues in your school, was your reaction the same as your parents, or was it the complete opposite? Many whites raised in the '40s and '50s became liberals in reaction to their parents' biased and segregated lives.

Facing your family history of prejudice—either as victims or oppressors—is not easy and can't be done in one sitting. All of us have a tendency to conveniently forget what is most painful. So, keep a written account of the answers you find. This journal will help when you need to be reminded of what you discovered. It will be a treasure to share with your children. Even if you're not particularly proud of your family's history, this undertaking can fuel your determination to make your children's future something to boast about.

6

Provide History That Fosters Pride

When eleven-year-old Charles is asked what he knows about his great-grandparents, he squirms in his chair, then mumbles, "Not much." How about his grandparents? Ah, his face lights up; he answers with gusto, "They came from Alabama and lived on a farm! I went there!"

Charles happens to be black, but that same proud reaction can come from a child of any race. Children take an interest in their family background, because it gives them a sense of identity and value. The same rewards can be reaped by studying the roots of culture and races. If children know where they have come from, what obstacles their ancestors have endured and conquered, what progress they have made over the centuries, they can't help but feel a sense of pride in their people.

Most parents don't have too much influence over the way teachers present history lessons. But you still can have a personal impact on your child's understanding of his ancestry and the history of his culture, as well as that of others. Here are some creative projects that can be done without too much effort and should be considered by families of all cultural backgrounds.

Display family photos from one and two generations ago, in full view for your child to see and contemplate. One woman puts her large collection of framed photos of relatives in the front hall on what she lovingly calls the ancestor table.

For your child's birthday, start the yearly tradition of giving him a book about his cultural history or a book by an author who's a member of his culture. This can be an especially meaningful gift for American parents to give to their foreign-born adopted child; such books help the child maintain a sense of connection with his native country.

Give or suggest books written by people of your culture about your culture. Read some of them with your child—this usually works up to age twelve. After that, continue to encourage your child to read such books. Make use of computer systems in the library or a book store to select from the hundreds of books now available.

Make a family tree. This can be a major project requiring a great deal of research and time, but it doesn't have to be done all at once. Instead, start by drawing a small tree that traces family lines as far as you can remember. Tack the tree up on your child's bedroom wall, or on the fridge door, so that referring to it becomes part of the family routine. For young children, put stickers or stars to mark special folks, or to show that they came from different parts of the country or world.

Whether you have small or major family reunions, make sure your child attends and actively participates. At the reunion, have a map of the U.S. or the world with pins locating where relatives came from. Older children can help by audio taping or video recording the older relatives reliving their memories. Get them talking about what race relations were like forty years ago. If you are forthright in this endeavor and interested, your children and other relatives will be, too.

Be sure to take your child along with you to family weddings, funerals and religious celebrations, where folks gather to mark a life passage. These rituals are family history in the making and will provide a sense of community your child will long remember.

Tell stories and ask others in the family to do the same. Let your child hear the myths and legends of your people as often as possible.

Watch movies or special television features on the history of your culture. An African American grandmother got on the phone and called all her friends and family to alert them to a television special on the black airmen who flew and fought in World War II. "It's important that our children know this story," she says. "All that our people hear is the negative. We need to know the positive, the accomplishments. We need to tell our children, 'You can't be dishonest, cheat or steal, because your people have paved the way; we have accomplished too much.' "

All races need to polish and preserve their family pride. Don't assume your child knows his heritage. He needs to be told that his great-grandfather struggled as a farmer in France, or that his great-great-grandmother died on the boat coming to this country. Children love to know about their roots; it not only fascinates them, it gives them a deep sense of pride.

7

Get the Whole Story—His-Story, Her Story, Their Story & Our Story

Reasonable people now agree that history, as it's taught in most American schools, is the story of our country and the wider world, told from the vantage point of the European American male. Recognizing and acknowledging that perspective was a big step forward for many of us. Then we seem to have stalled.

So minority parents—and others who hold multicultural values—continue to find a need to broaden our children's viewpoint with additional readings and lessons. Boston University education professor Vivian R. Johnson tells a tale from her childhood, about her first collision with "his-story," that shows how meaningful such extracurricular instruction can be.

She was an African American child of about twelve, growing up in Los Angeles, when a white teacher plowed into a period of history—the Civil War and its aftermath—

that was crucial and defining to both of their cultures.

Johnson soon after came home from school repeating a version of the past that virtually canonized white men for freeing the slaves. Johnson's astonished mother handed her W. E. B. Du Bois' *Black Reconstruction in America* and sat her down to read. That classic history of the years 1860–1880 details the decisive role played by African Americans in forcing the abolition of slavery and in restoring the Union. It's a chapter of history that is diminished, if not outright omitted, by mainstream accounts.

Despite some minor factual errors and conceptual flaws, Du Bois' pioneering work of 1935 transformed the way historians interpret the Civil War period, according to historian David Levering Lewis, author of a Pulitzer Prize–winning biography of Du Bois. *Black Reconstruction* recounted events from an African American perspective, including Du Bois' contention that slaves were instrumental in causing the collapse of the Confederacy by quitting the fields and crippling the Southern plantation economy. That left rebels with the choice of surrendering to the North or to 4 million former slaves, who presumably would win either way.

With Du Bois under her belt, Johnson returned to class, determined to set the record straight. "I talked about how black people liberated themselves," she said, "stating facts that were foreign to the teacher."

Johnson brought the book with her and could point to the page where Du Bois said: "The North was not Abolitionist. It was overwhelmingly in favor of Negro slavery, so long as this did not interfere with Northern moneymaking. But, on the other hand, there was a minority of the North who hated slavery with perfect hatred. . . . As the Abolition-democracy gained in prestige and power, they appeared as prophets, and led by statesmen, they began to guide the nation out of the morass into which it had fallen."

Furthermore, Du Bois argued, it wasn't virtue that turned the tide toward abolition in the end so much as it was the weight of world opinion. "[U]nless the North faced the world with the moral strength of declaring openly that they were fighting for the emancipation of slaves," Du Bois wrote, "they would probably find that the world would recognize the South as a separate nation; that ports would be opened; that trade would begin; and that despite all the military advantage of the North, the war would be lost."

The teacher was not impressed by Du Bois or by Johnson's assertiveness. "I can remember being very hurt," she says, "because I was a very good student and a well-behaved young woman. . . . My grandfather consoled me and tried explaining why that information was upsetting to people. I remember asking a thousand different ways: 'If it was factual, why would people be upset?'. . . I kept coming back to it, weeks later, because I didn't understand. . . . My grandfather talked about white guilt and how some people really are sorry for what happened but don't know what to do about it, so they just want it all to go away. . . . I now see that he wanted to help me understand racism as a flaw in American society."

Parents need to encourage their children to explore and compare the views that various peoples have of themselves, of history, of life. Once such seeds of diversity are planted, once children learn to accept and respect the existence of many different perspectives—all of which have inconsistencies, if not absolute contradictions—they are more likely to continue seeking the big picture as they voyage through life.

See that your children study the histories of many cultures—especially those of their fellow citizens. Start with biographies that are both engaging and educational. They are available now for nearly all ages and reading levels.

8

Make History a Healing Course

Minorities aren't the only ones who are hurt by inaccurate or selective accounts of history. An African American college professor tells us that some of his white students also are offended when they discover how much was left out of their grade-school lessons.

"They feel hoodwinked," says Joseph Windham, who teaches history at the Northern Virginia Community College. After attending his multiculturally oriented classes, students often look back on their first history and social studies courses and feel manipulated.

They see how they missed certain fundamentals because schools taught them history as the acts of "a few good men." Or because they sat through years of *"Jeopardy* history" classes, memorizing dates and events without much background or context. And because the contributions made by peoples of color tended to be downplayed, if noted at all.

That's after the light dawns, though. At first, Windham's students of World Civilization—an introductory history course stretching from the beginnings of civilization through medieval times—will frown and raise their hands to say things like "That's not the way I learned it." They're skeptical, the professor says, and have their antennae up to catch any cultural bias there might be in his presentation.

"But I don't come off with any heavy Afrocentric interpretation," he says. "I talk about the development of humanity chronologically, looking at the contributions made by the various peoples who fit into that chronology. . . . So they come to respect and acknowledge how humanity began in Africa. Not because I made it happen that way—but because that's how it happened."

Students enter his class having heard about the Rift Valley or having seen *National Geographic* specials on the origins of the species. But they've never had the facts presented to them quite so. "Anytime you start talking about Africa being significant, it's controversial," Windham says.

"People just aren't used to hearing it."

He goes back through history on a *Roots* journey that leaves no doubt about Africa being everyone's motherland. But as soon as his students become clear on that point, they begin puzzling over why a civilization—the Western one— would so virulently and persistently reject and disown its own source.

The professor has to use scientific magazines, historical journal articles and slide shows during the early phases of the course because textbooks generally don't delve into ancient African history. "They tend to be Eurocentric," Windham says. "They'll start with the Tigris and Euphrates. Maybe mention Egypt. But they won't emphasize what we know about Africa, especially when it comes to defining culture and civilization."

Not that Windham stresses any particular continent or culture, either. He simply credits each for what it has given the world, how it has contributed to the whole. Once his students realize how much is missing from their textbooks, they start thinking back over their schooling and see a pattern of instruction that emphasized people's differences rather than their commonalities. And then they get angry.

"They get so angry that I've got to pull them out of it, because they'll stop learning and just focus on their resentment," the professor says.

The students, who are mostly from working-class families and are putting themselves through school, start becoming more conscious of racial prejudice and try to pinpoint its origins. They also come to see how many conflicts in history that are blamed on race are really more rooted in struggles over wealth, power and politics.

In American history, for example, they learn that before the Civil War, only 8,000 white men were rich enough to live the legend we asociate with the Old South—occupying huge plantations that were maintained by hundreds of slaves. That tiny minority dominated the South and owned half of its 4 million slaves. But the other half of Dixie's human chattel was owned in twos and threes by some of the 2 million whites who worked small farms, often right alongside their slaves. Some 5 million other Southern whites were dirt poor and largely illiterate.

The students then start to wander in their wonder. They try to figure out why so many white Americans cry during *Gone with the Wind*, as if their forebears once reclined on Southern verandas, with mint juleps in hand. They take another look at their picture of the Old South and question whether it was truly that glamorous and grand. And they ask to be reminded why the tenacity of the Confederacy should be saluted?

They marvel at the myth and how it has obscured similarities between the hardships whites and blacks historically have suffered. And as the term progresses, the professor says, exchanges between students of differing races become more natural and less guarded.

"It's not like they start walking around together whistling and holding hands," says Windham. "But they're on the same path."

9

Sensitize Your Parent-School Organization

In the heart of Milwaukee, a group of ten mothers met for two hours and learned a great deal from one another about the racial tension in their middle school; some of it was heartening, much of it was upsetting, but the mothers, all members of the parent-school organization, were game to work further on the problems. They also got to know one another on a more personal level. "We should do this more often—and make it mandatory!" said one woman, good humoredly, as she left. "If parents don't show up, they get expelled, or at least get put on probation."

One of the most effective ways to make and maintain relationships with diverse groups of people, and to meet the needs of the multicultural community in your school, is to participate actively in your parent-school organization.

It's not enough to pay your dues. You have to attend meetings, volunteer for activities, make phone calls, contribute ideas and make yourself known and heard. Recent studies

show that after a child turns ten, parents participate less in the child's activities; and yet parental involvement is crucial at the middle school and high school level, when your child needs your power of advocacy for a quality education.

Sensitize your parent-school organization to the multicultural interests of the student body. A growing number of parent-school organizations are offering conflict resolution programs and workshops on multiculturalism. Form groups to discuss racial and cultural issues in the school, such as how to teach history more inclusively and how to respond to self-segregation. Take an anonymous poll and ask the parents which racial issues they'd like to talk about in workshops and small discussion groups.

Suggest that your parent-school organization schedule their meetings and workshops on Saturdays—a much needed arrangement for working parents.

Assure attendance by providing free child care during meetings. Middle school or high school teens can watch younger children in another room.

Provide language translation for non-English–speaking parents at meetings and workshops. This can be done in conjunction with the school's language department, using students or other parents who are adept in two languages. This is especially important on the back-to-school evenings, when foreign-born parents may be uncertain whether they should attend. Send a flier or news note well beforehand, or at registration, letting parents who aren't fluent in English know that translations will be available throughout the school year.

Raise funds or solicit donations to buy books on race and multiculturalism for the school library. Assign a committee of parents to choose those books that best suit your student body.

Decide if uniforms may help your school reduce gang recognition and social discrimination. Provide a means of

sponsorship or support for families who can not afford uniforms.

Suggest a visitor's service—parents who call on a new student's home to meet the parents and answer any questions they may have about the school. The visiting parents may volunteer or earn a small wage taken from the parent-school organization's budget; several schools that use this method employ grandparents, who often have more time than working parents do. This program is especially helpful when new immigrants are matched with a parent who speaks their native language.

Schools have been promoting parental involvement for generations. What makes it different and imperative now are the special needs of the multicultural school community, which can not be ignored without jeopardizing the quality of education your child and others deserve.

10

Involve the Community

"**W**e can't do this alone" is the complaint of many parents, who feel overwhelmed by the weight and enormity of the iniquities that face their children every single day. "Parents expect too much from us" is the cry of teachers and principals, who are exhausted and disappointed by their efforts to combat insidious racism in school halls and classrooms.

It's true, we can't do it alone. Our society has created this mess, and it's going to take a good chunk of the society to straighten it out. It is also true that in this day and age, the task of teaching fairness and making it a reality that sticks is not a one-person job done in the privacy of the home. Parents can preach and be the best of role models, but they compete with the powerful influences of the media, peers and other adults who speak persuasive, dramatic languages of generalization and prejudice.

It used to be that everyone in a neighborhood joined together to serve as the conscience and watchdog of their children. Scores of adults, from all races, told Barbara stories of how when they were teenagers their parents always knew what trouble they were in, or even thinking about, before they came in the door. "My father was always called by this one guy who lived down the block, and I don't know how he knew what I was up to," laughs one black man, who says he wishes he could as easily keep tabs on his own kids. There used to be an unquestioned code of respect and responsibility that emanated from the community. For some it came from the church folk or the congregation; for others it was one, two or three blocks of neighbors who knew and loved everyone's children. No longer is there this collective caring and con- science-making. With job transiency, the rise of single-parent homes and the general isolation of our busy lives, we've lost our connection with others and convinced ourselves that we're fighting these battles all alone.

But it doesn't have to be that way. Some parents are reach- ing out to the community for creative ideas and skills that can shape an atmosphere of fairness for their children. Consider adopting some of their tactics as your own:

Minority-owned businesses that provide internships and incentives to do better in school;

Professionals who provide mentoring on a regular basis to high school students interested in a particular field;

Business associations that fund diversity workshop train- ing of students;

Retired teachers who offer after-school and evening tutor- ing programs for students to bring grades and skills up so they can enter honors programs;

Communications firms that give free press advice and place positive news and feature stories about school efforts to diversify and to combat racism;

Community colleges, local colleges and universities that set up joint programs for diversity or for problem solving techniques. Also, college students who major in foreign languages and assist in the school orientation of immigrant parents;

Retirees and school alumnae from the community who serve as home visitors to explain to parents the various programs and options available to the students;

Churches, synagogues and colleges that provide the facilitators and facilities for open forums, or workshops, where there is a dialogue among races; and

Local radio and television stations that schedule talk shows on racial issues.

Call on the aid of churches, synagogues, professional organizations or local business bureaus for help. The more people you have pitching in, the more creativity and energy you'll have—meaning you should get the job done more quickly and effectively than if you try to do it alone. Community effort also gives the kids the message that this is a very serious situation, that things must change for the better and that you do care.

11

Begin the Lessons Early, Teach Responsibility

There is a distinct and telling difference as to when and how white parents and minority parents talk to their children about race. Whites typically touch on the subject when their children are in elementary school, or even as late as middle school. Approaches and words may vary from family to family, but more than likely the white parents' lessons about color and human dignity are given infrequently, and only when provoked by some racial incident the child has observed in school or on television. Little wonder that whites are often surprised to learn that many minority parents continually talk about the problems and politics of color with their children, starting at age two-and-a half or three, without mincing words or talking down. According to one black father of two: "We talk to our kids about color early because it's a matter of survival, as preparation to go out in the real world. Our parents articulated that we had to be twice as good, work twice as hard in order to be accepted. I tell my son and daughter the same thing."

Whenever Barbara met with parents to discuss the different ways they talk to their children, white parents invariably posed two questions to minority parents: Doesn't your message just perpetuate the polarization between whites and minorities? Doesn't it create a negative mind-set for your children?

"It does polarize," answered one black parent of teenagers. "But it's the only way that you can protect your kids so that when they grow up they understand that it's not a fair playing ground. There are always going to be a few people who slip through who will find themselves on a level playing ground, but ninety-nine percent of the people of color do not."

As for the negative mind-set, many minority parents said that they give realistic, protective advice, but they add to the message the element of responsibility. All of us are responsible for our future no matter what our color, creed or economic lot in life, a father preaches to his family. He also tells them how they each have to participate more fully in eliminating the division between the races. That's a tall order for a youngster, but if it's told over and over, this father believes it will take hold. As another African American father of four says: "I tell my children, 'Look, be very good at what you do. I want you to aspire. I want you to play fair, be honest. I want you to be successful. But understand that when you don't achieve success, it's not necessarily about you.' "

He goes on to tell his children: "You can't fly off the handle and become just another angry black, a statistic in crime. And you can't just think that things are just going to happen, good or bad. You have to come together with other people to work on the problems of racism." It's a message he has been giving his two oldest kids, now just out of college, since the time they were little; and he's still giving it to his two younger children who are going into middle school.

A Peruvian mother says that her two young teenagers have run into prejudice from both their black and their white classmates at their private school in Washington, D.C. The situation angers and saddens her, particularly because the problem isn't publicly recognized by the school community. Convinced that she shouldn't gloss over or deny the fact of racism to her children, she works on their resilience. "A balanced parent will let their child know that they will come across situations where there is no explanation except bias," she explains. "But they must be told that they can manage in such a setting, and that's a reality."

Some minority parents may argue that it's not a reality—indeed, they believe that it's impossible to manage in this white, biased world. If they keep giving that message, however, their children will feel no impetus to try. All parents, whether minority or majority, have to break the pattern of defeatism by encouraging the next generation to make a difference by speaking out against racism and by broadening their multicultural relationships. And white parents need to start delivering that message to their children consistently and at a much younger age. Preferably, these are lessons that they'll teach by example, as well as with words.

Infancy Through Preschool

It is about midway through this initial period of miraculously fast-paced development that most children first notice the many variations in skin tone and eye color and hair texture and facial features that exist among the people they encounter in the course of a day. You can follow their eyes, or the reach of their chubby hands, and see them taking inventory—at the supermarket, in the doctor's office, on the bus, at the dinner table.

It is also then that children begin to absorb the values of those who are closest to them. Parents—as well as others who nurture our children—often transfer to them deeply rooted biases that we hold toward one type of people, or against another. We deliver a lot of this basic training unthinkingly, automatically. Other times we do it more deliberately and justifiably—in showing our children how to identify and avoid those who may do them harm, for example. Consider how easily and naturally it begins—the way we teach children to discriminate, to tell the difference between friend and foe.

For the first eight months of life, your baby concentrates on learning her own little body, its parts and the rudiments of how they work. After that, a good deal of her curiosity is directed outward—toward other people, the world and its wonders.

As she gains control over her legs and toddles forth, your child becomes as free as she is ever likely to be. And that independence is joyful, exhilarating. She'll thrill at her newfound ability to govern herself, deciding to propel herself in one direction at one moment, and another in the next. Her choices reveal her mind to be as open as her whim is flexible.

At this age, your child is an explorer. Everything is new, and she wants to check it all out. As she investigates, she forms her first opinions. She begins to bring order to her world by roughly ranking and classifying the people and things that she encounters. Her preferences, at this point, are purely hers—unsullied by whatever preceded her arrival on this Earth.

She gravitates toward certain objects, foods and individuals simply because she is attracted to them. She sizes them up by how they feel, taste and react. Then, gradually, she begins to factor into her assessments certain cues that you give her. For as eager as she is to venture out into the unknown, she'll also be depending on you, or her care provider, to serve as her net. As self-reliant as she seems to want to be, she'll have an ear out to hear murmurs of your encouragement when she encounters something or someone you consider to be a safe target for her curiosity. And she'll get used to heeding your warnings when she heads for something or someone you deem to be dangerous or inappropriate.

So be careful how you judge, and make sure your criteria are sound. As she goes about organizing and categorizing her adventures, she is likely to be making heavy use of your filing system. And years later she may not consciously remember why she rejects or excludes a certain kind of people, or when it was that she began to scorn the way they look or talk, the kinds of food they eat, how they dress—even the sorts of sounds they make as they celebrate, worship or simply commune in a family setting.

Whether it was your intention to bequeath your biases or not, your child adopts your leanings and, according to them, begins to pre-judge people. The boon is that she will welcome into her world most of those people she senses that you accept and respect. And if you surround her with a core group that is varied in hue and ethnicity, then she will launch her life's journey with a solid sense of belonging to the ever-growing multicultural nature of our nation. As she begins to teethe and talk, she also will be cultivating a confidence in herself of the sturdiest, healthiest kind—that which is rooted in respect for others.

12

Teach Identity Through Comparison

You can both widen a child's world and sharpen his view of self with a diverse group of playmates and the comparisons to one another that they will naturally make. A child first focuses on the range of our racial differences when he is about two years old. That's when he is cobbling together an identity for himself, so it's natural for him to inspect others. Likewise, he is busy noting gender. He's trying to figure out where and how he stands in relation to the rest of his world—positions that can't be pointed out by any parent's compass. Your child needs to sort these things out for himself, mainly by observing and interacting with others. You can help, however, by supplying the tools and a supportive, but relaxed, setting.

If your child isn't yet in daycare or preschool, consider putting together a playgroup or having him join an existing one that is diverse in membership and that meets twice a week or so. Exposure to other children at this point will help develop his social skills, in any event. But beyond that, it simply makes sense for your child—while he is engaged in this process of finding and securing his racial and ethnic identity—to be surrounded by a realistic representation of his fellow citizens.

Think about it. You are limiting your child's potential if you restrict his vision. Don't hamper him with social blinders. Give your child a free, fair vision of the world, with all of its colors and cultures. Give him a chance to more accurately and completely define himself, to see himself in many contexts.

You can choose a playgroup for him that is balanced ethnically and racially or one that is weighted to offset a majority race or ethnicity in your neighborhood. However you choose to structure the group, if the children are not only strangers, but are foreign to one another's ways, it makes sense to have them meet on neutral ground, especially in the beginning. Otherwise, those children who are familiar with the setting may dominate, while others feel out of place and hold themselves back. Choose a park, for example. Some public libraries welcome small groups for story hours, after which you can serve a snack. Don't allow a structured activity to defeat the purpose of your playgroup, however. Ideally, the children should interact with one another, more so than with adults. Also, remember their short attention span at this age.

Once you get your child's group up and going, try not to hover. Sit back and let the children do most of the rest. If they are given a level playground from the beginning, they'll be less likely to copy the nonsensical color-based biases that we have.

If you don't have existing contacts with families in other communities, you can post notices in churches, temples, mosques, and schools, inviting parents interested in reaching out culturally to contact you. Also, consider sounding out your co-workers.

Hear a word of caution, however, from a black middle-class mother in Atlanta who sees too many playgroups being organized mainly as political or professional networks for parents—or as social laboratories where black children are much outnumbered and assigned the role of guinea pig. "I think you've got to be careful about those kinds of, quote, opportunities," she says. "They're always going to be there. Our children need to learn first that what they've got is good and that they don't have to apologize to anybody. We shouldn't have to bend over backwards to be an integrationalist or a multiculturalist."

This mother's position is a common one among African Americans. She resents the extra steps her children must take toward the middle, yet she knows she must eventually push them in that direction if they are not to be marginalized. And so the conundrum continues.

13

Reflect Reality Through Mirrors, Art and Yourself

Don't think that it's vain to put a mirror on the wall of your child's bedroom. There should be mirrors at her preschool, too. Seeing her image reflected at this age is not going to make her conceited. Children need to become comfortable with their appearance now. Without going overboard, of course, they should feel good about the way they look. It's key to their self-confidence.

Parents can help by regularly praising children's strong suits—complimenting a son's delightfully curly hair, a daughter's beautiful brown skin, a cousin's friendly freckles.

Minority parents especially should surround their children with joyful images of people who resemble them and who differ from the regimental European American profiles that march so relentlessly through our media. Hang family portraits—both of ancestors and newcomers—prominently on your walls.

Launch a photography collection with your child, featuring your culture's most admirable achievers. Accumulate it casually or methodically, according to your inclination and the age of your child. But don't fall into the trap of portraying those men and women exclusively as icons or as martyrs to be mourned. Teach the history and honor the heroes, but celebrate their humanity as well. Find photos of them with their families or ones that show their humor. Make them accessible as models for our children.

Subscribe to magazines that present a range of cultures on their pages. You don't have to leave them in reach of your four-year-old to "read" at will. You can have her help you disassemble old issues, though, pulling out pictures that portray minorities in jobs and roles that are seldom seen on television or in your neighborhood. Then tape those photos to the wall at the level of your child's eye.

You can make a similar display with photos of artwork from various parts of the world. Experiment by posting them in pairs—hanging pieces from Picasso's cubist period, for example, next to some of the African sculpture that inspired him. Your child is likely to be intrigued by patterns at this age but is unlikely to see such a combination elsewhere. There's no telling whether or where the visual cultural linkages you lay out for her now will surface in the future. But we know that art has great capacities to heal and to unify.

Once your child has a solid sense of self and pride in her own people, it will be easier for her to find joy in the differences of others. Without that base—that emotional home plate—a minority child can be conned by commercial stereotypes into rejecting herself.

In terms of appearance, mainstream white America most values people who are blond, have blue eyes and are thin. The more people differ from that ideal, the more they tend to be devalued. So if black children are to feel good about the way they look, their parents and elders and others who care must maintain a separate world where more familiar and friendly values prevail. Either that or children will be tempted to change their look. Their natural desire to appear attractive to others prompts them to do unnatural things to themselves.

White standards of beauty are so powerfully and pervasively marketed that they seduce virtually everyone at some point. But those standards are not, nor should they be, the measure of us all. Often it falls to our children to voice that reality—or to act it out—before parents relinquish their fantasies.

An African American Ivy League–educated lawyer from Indianapolis tells of how her two-year-old daughter came home from her predominantly black preschool one day and said, "I don't want to be brown anymore." The mother, who had taken to wearing "fun" tinted contact lenses that made her eyes look hazel instead of their natural brown, immediately popped out the lenses. That was her first reaction to her daughter's self-rejection. Next, the mother wondered whether she should stop using chemicals to straighten her curly hair, whether she should simply wear it as nature made it.

The mother is glib and almost amusing as she tells the story, reeling off the reasons she sees no harm in black people wanting to look different. She obviously has delivered this little spiel before. Black people are instinctively artistic, she says. They're aesthetically restless, deeply into fashion and its flair. That's why we often change aspects of our appearance so drastically. So frequently. So constantly. The mother pauses, then continues haltingly. She describes how odd she felt watching her daughter groping for someone else's image. Then she concludes that what her daughter really needs to see in her mother is a reflection of herself.

14

Select the Right Preschool for Your Child

Most parents are not bewildered by a multitude of marvelous choices when it comes to selecting a preschool or finding a solution to daycare. Our country has a long way to go before it adequately meets the early developmental needs of our children. It's little surprise, then, that parents who have the most financial flexibility also have the most options.

In making your choice—as limited or as broad as it may be—we encourage you to consider a multicultural setting. The sooner children learn to get along with others, the more likely they will be able as adults to nurse our nation's racial wounds back to health.

We must urge you also to consider, however, that it is often white children who most stand to gain from diversity during the preschool years, and minorities who most risk losing. This is especially true in schools or daycare centers where minorities are grossly outnumbered.

The primary judgment the parent of any child needs to make in evaluating a preschool is whether it will provide a nurturing and supportive atmosphere that affirms the child's developing identity. If you are a European American, chances are your children encounter powerful images every day that reflect and reinforce positive aspects of your people. By such means, their self-image is suitably strengthened. By the same token, without extensive or realistic contact with other races and cultures, white children are likely to absorb the media's many negative and ham-handed stereotypes of non-whites.

If you're an African American, your children are more likely to catch glimpses of themselves in the shadows of our society. Or held up for ridicule, as black sitcom characters too often are. Your children see people who look like them demeaned. At the same time, they see white people championed, held up as the ultimate of everything. And those visions scroll past your children each time they step away from your embrace to walk in the world or watch TV—perhaps even when they dream. Those images are so dominant in America that they are practically inescapable.

Given the luxury of choice, therefore, many minority parents judiciously send their children to preschools where the majority of students and teachers share their race or ethnicity. Such places tend to fortify and secure children's individual as well as cultural identities, thereby better preparing them for the inevitable harsh realities of racism.

"I have seen too many instances where 'the only black child' has been seriously damaged," says Louise Derman-Sparks, a European American teacher and veteran activist for diversity and social justice in early-childhood education. Minority parents should be wary, she says, of essentially sacrificing their children to situations where they will be lone specimens for the education and exposure of whites. Minority parents who choose not to make their children ambassadors of multiculturalism during these early years figure that grade school is soon enough for them to be plunged into white America's mainstream and feel first-hand its inherent arrogance and disdain for other cultures. The counter-argument to this approach, of course, is that racism is unlikely to retreat dramatically enough in our lifetimes to put off preparing our children to deal with it.

No route is perfect. Sending a minority child to a school where he is in the majority is no guarantee that he will be bathed in warm praise and approbation. He could be assigned a minority teacher who has internalized racism in such a way to mirror society's attitudes and reinforce its negative images of the child. As twisted as this scenario may seem, it is unfortunately common and to be guarded against.

As for white children, because they get such steady streams of positive reinforcement from so many sources, it would be difficult to injure their identities simply by enrolling them at a diverse preschool. If anything, white children are likely to gain from the experience. So send them to multicultural schools—that is, if you can find ones, or form ones, with enough minority children in attendance to make a mix that's healthy for all concerned.

"Studies have now proven, pretty much beyond a doubt, that racism is damaging to people who practice it," says Derman-Sparks, who is based at California's Pacific Oaks College and who developed an increasingly popular "Anti-Bias Curriculum" for preschools. Racism creates a "toxic environment" both for the perpetrators and the victims.

Regardless of race, the sad reality is that most parents choose a preschool or a daycare facility primarily according to its proximity to work or home and its affordability. They consider themselves lucky if they find a place that matches those two needs and that also seems unlikely to do their children any harm.

Remember that whatever degree of diversity a school has, you can always bolster it by signing your child up for a playgroup that either emphasizes his culture or broadens his appreciation of others.

15

Don't Pretend Discrimination Doesn't Exist

Face it: Race-based discrimination is as American as apple pie. Don't tell your children that color "doesn't matter." Don't lead them to believe that people are "the same," whether they are "red, white, yellow, green or blue." It's simply not true. We aren't all "the same."

If your end goal is for your children to treat all people fairly, then say so, and be clear about it. That's an admirable objective. However, don't make the common mistake of thinking we can solve our racial problems by decree—that if only we decided not to notice them anymore, they wouldn't exist.

It may seem noble to strive toward a colorblind society, but it's misguided. And even if we set out as a nation aiming for that state of sameness, we'd have to mend many historical fences and bridge a modern-day abyss before arriving. Racism is too deeply rooted in our culture to pretend it away.

Tactics aside, let's reconsider the goal. Should we really want to be blind to our differences? It's undeniable that they have periodically fractured our society in ways that were bitter, bloody and costly. But the creative and ingenious culture that continues to spring from our diversity also enriches us. Moreover, that manic and magical thing that we make when combined may well be the sinew that holds us together as a nation. We wouldn't be able to tell that for sure, of course, until it was past worth knowing.

On a smaller scale, consider the price individuals would pay for such a policy of sameness. A colorblind society would make many aspects of our selves superfluous. It would diminish us to deny our cultural, ethnic and racial differences. The melting pot provides tidy democratic solutions only in our myths. In real life, the dominant culture prevails, while the others simmer away.

If you truly believe in equity, as opposed to might making right, consider teaching your child that sometimes we have to treat people differently in order to be fair. Children even out differences between themselves all the time and will grasp this concept immediately. Don't worry now about filling them in on the grisly historical details of why certain people have been wronged. You can do that when they're a little older.

Also, children tend to be very literal, especially when talking to adults about supposedly serious issues. And because they know that real people don't have skin colors like those found in a rainbow, or in a crayon box, you may effectively trivialize the subject of race by saying that it makes no difference if a person is black or blue.

On the other hand, don't be so guarded about what you say that the subject becomes taboo. Especially since, as we noted earlier, children start cataloging skin color at the tender age of two. That's also when they begin to perceive, in very general terms, that people have different lots in life, often according to their color. As children sort through all the new data that swamps them during these early years, they tend to associate various types of people with their habitat or the context in which they're encountered. It's natural.

A four-year-old white boy sees a tall black man shopping at a supermarket in a suburb of Dallas. The boy asks his father which "TV [basketball] team" the man plays for. A four-year-old Anglo-American girl in Los Angeles comes home from her first day of preschool and says there's a "little maid" in her class. She is referring to a Mexican American, whose cultural kin the Anglo girl sees up close only when they come to clean her family's house. The parents of both of these children consider themselves to be colorblind and claim to have been stymied when they tried to figure out how their kids made such assumptions about minorities encountered "out of context." But the kids weren't to blame.

Scenarios similar to those above occur so commonly in life that comedians tell variations of them on late-night TV. And we laugh at them! Perhaps to keep from crying at the absurdity of our apartheid. Let's use them, instead, as reasons to reject colorblindness as a tactic. After all, if it doesn't work on children, who are we fooling?

Let's not pretend there's no discrimination in our world. It lives and breathes right alongside us, and we should all recognize it and dedicate ourselves to its demise.

16

Rise to the Challenge at School

A black mother of two who had just moved to a midsized Midwestern town told us of her search for a good public school with a diverse student body. She visited a model magnet school where classes were carefully balanced by race. The principal took the mother to see one of the kindergarten classes her daughter would be assigned to the next year if she attended. The principal, who was white, cooed as she entered the classroom, "All these little black faces, all these little white faces, little brown faces—they're all so beautiful!" The mother said she cringed and thought to herself, "Oh, that is so fake."

The mother asked the principal, who otherwise came across as very professional and efficient, how many black teachers were on the faculty. The principal parried the question pleasantly, saying, "You know, I don't really know. I don't keep track."

The mother said she thought to herself, "That's such a stupid remark. Of course she knows." The mother kept her thoughts to herself, however, and sent her children to the school because it ended up being the best option available.

Now we don't know whether the principal knew the racial breakdown of her faculty or whether she was truly so impartial that when she envisioned her staff, she didn't see their color. We do know, however, that the mother didn't believe she should risk finding out.

We can't advise you to act in ways that are honorable in theory but harmful to your child in practice. Nor would we expect you to follow such advice. There comes a point, however, when we must examine the benefits of going along to get along. For travel serves no purpose if you never reach your destination.

Instead of challenging the school system and its administrators to find out how much of their seeming commitment to diversity was window-dressing and how much was real, our Midwestern mother bit her tongue. She and her husband elected to exert more subtle sorts of pressure. They are both well-educated, have white-collar jobs and "make it a point to wear suits and carry our briefcases to make it clear that we have high expectations," the mother said, whenever they have cause to meet with their children's teachers or principal. "It's like putting on armor," said the children's father. It's a civil show of force intended to discourage outright attacks. It's a salute to uniformity, a way of signaling shared values. Can that be enough to protect our children? Or to promote their best interests?

This is such a strange time for our country. We want so badly to believe we have settled our racial accounts. If that is so, then why can't we openly consider the ramifications of our past without fear of sparking new reprisals? Why can't we see each other for who and what we are? Why should we have to sugarcoat people in order to see them as equals? Why should we avoid acknowledging the differences among our racial characteristics? Our identities?

Why can't we be home free? Because freedom simply isn't free. "If there is no struggle, there is no progress," Frederick Douglass said nearly a century and a half ago. "Power concedes nothing without a demand. It never did and it never will."

While it may be ill-advised to tackle the school system single-handedly, it may be time for parents who are dedicated to diversity to stand together and ask for an accounting. Is your school diverse in skin tone only? Does it appear to be multicultural while offering a menu restricted to mainstream choices?

You may find that the spirit of a school's diversity needs to be rekindled as regularly as its student body turns over. And it may be your turn to stoke the fire.

17

Forge Ahead Without Hindering Your Child

It was springtime, when working parents wake up to the fact that the school year is coming to an end and they need to figure out how their child will spend the long summer days. Mary Ann was canvassing camps and summer schools, trying to find programs that would be both good for her son, Scotty, and good to him. She sought places that would keep his mind as well as his muscles limber during the break from school and that would nourish his ever-evolving sense of self.

She asked for suggestions from friends who had children a little older than Scotty and had recently enrolled in programs that were suitable or not. She went through as many area listings of camps and summer-school programs as she could find. Not many locales have comprehensive guides. You may find guides to segments of the summer market—such as programs run by private, church-affiliated schools. Or you may find guides that are good for comparing, say, the mix of academics and sports offered by various programs. If they mention diversity at all, most guides simply state a catchall disclaimer assuring parents that its schools "do not discriminate on the basis of race, color, national or ethnic origin."

What does that mean? There's no telling. You can try to get the racial breakdown of the faculty and student body. That's hard to do on the phone, however. You're likely to get transferred five times and put on hold for 15 minutes while administrators try to ascertain your motive. We Americans are so paranoid about race that it seems we presume no question on the subject to be innocent.

In any event, the numbers are just a clue to how hospitable a school or camp might be to your child's cultural identity. As a kind of safeguard, we recommend taking your child for a visit. No matter how good a place sounds or looks on paper, if the chemistry's not right, nothing may go right.

At the first camp Mary Ann and her son visited—which ironically ended up being the one they liked most—Mary Ann asked the director what the ratio of the races was among her students. The director looked flustered and sputtered something about not being sure offhand. "But it's not a problem!" she blurted out. Scotty, who had been busy exploring a classroom while the women paused to talk, was startled and puzzled by the sudden tone of denial and defensiveness in the director's voice. He turned toward them, all ears.

Mary Ann was steaming. "It may not be a problem for you," she managed to say evenly, before proceeding to explain why many African Americans feel they must be vigilant about such balances and influences on their children. She tried to use words that would be convincing to the director but not alarming to Scotty. It wasn't easy, but it turned out being worthwhile, as Scotty had a happy and productive summer at the camp. The director's initial bluster softened, the teachers were broad-minded, and the curriculum was strong. Mary Ann also was able to recruit children from several other African American families to attend, which boosted the camp's slim roll of minority students.

In laying the foundation for our children's future, those of us who value diversity often must be cool and controlled about it. We find ourselves walking a thin line between justice and civility. We must do the right thing—and fight the wrongs—without being too offensive about it. Righteous indignation all too often gets us nowhere today, given our country's current hypocritical state of denial regarding race. Unless, of course, we join together and become a force for change.

Individually, we can't always be on guard. And we won't always be emotionally prepared when we're challenged to diversity duels. We may not have it in us to respond delicately or diplomatically. We may react more naturally. The unfortunate result is that when we blow our stacks—no matter how justifiably—we often blow opportunities along with them. It's sad, but true.

The Early Elementary School Years

This is the age when children become chums, when they cease modeling themselves after their parents so much and shift a lot of their attentions and loyalties to friends instead. This is also when children first segregate themselves. They sort themselves out for natural and healthy reasons that reflect their strengths and weaknesses, their quirks and their conformities. They come together around any one or combination of their commonalities. Race doesn't have to be a determining factor in this process of defining self and selecting a core group, but it often is, simply because of the prominence our society accords it.

Innocence about race ends during these years and is never completely recovered. Whereas children began noticing our variations in skin tone long before now, most didn't attach any great significance to our differences. Now it becomes obvious that they mean a great deal—that skin colors are like codes, denoting rank and even fate.

Some children—both black and white—get very angry with this realization, although they may not be able to explain their reaction to you, or even to themselves. Others—especially minorities—begin a lifelong pattern of retreat, which may be just barely discernible at this stage but which is rationally based on their understanding that the game is rigged.

Kids want to belong now. To what, it almost doesn't matter, as long as they are with others who are like them. Some coalesce in the center around conventional achievers, while others drift toward irregular types on the fringes. The groups are tough in manner, or mild; charismatic or coy. Some have secret codes, while others wear readily identifiable signs of alliance. Groups form around their talents in the arts, as well as their abilities in sports. Some operate loosely, others hierarchically.

Children choose one kind of group over another according to their personality, and the kind of grounding they've gotten at home. They also may be heavily influenced by their sense of how much opportunity exists in the world for them, how great the chances are that they'll be able to succeed. For this is also a time when kids are learning the rules. They already know a good deal about categories and systems and how to classify things and people. Now, however, they begin to pick up the reasoning behind particular groupings. And they're starting to understand, regardless of how logical or foolish that reasoning may be, that the lines of life's classifications are not easily changed.

This can be a stunning discovery, say, for a black child who is used to playing with a group of white kids who haven't paid that much attention to color before now. In a blink, race and ethnicity are suddenly the determinants of inclusion or exclusion for the all-powerful group.

There's not much a parent can do to alter playground politics that turn on such divisions, except to hope that an observant teacher will weigh in, or that the child will talk at home about such incidents so that the parent can help him put things in perspective.

The ways in which a child now learns the basic patterns of life's rules will form the foundation of his morals. If he gets burned repeatedly while acting in good faith, his judgment of others may be forever negatively affected. Similarly, if a child is not admonished for selfish or harmful acts during this period, he may grow up with a false sense of privilege.

As parents, perhaps we can conduct initiation rites of our own during this time of our children's development. We can teach them to be inclusive when it comes to race—or at least teach them not to use race as an automatic basis for exclusion. It's fine for children to focus on tight groups and narrow interests now. That is their nature. We, however, have a duty to engage our children in larger rituals of fairness and justice, repeating them faithfully until they become second nature. For without such fundamentals, our children may proceed to amass power, but they are unlikely to ever know peace.

18

Tell the Truth About Slavery

It was February—the month we celebrate the birthday of Abraham Lincoln and the history of the people he "freed." Mary Ann's son, Scotty, was five years old, in kindergarten at a public school in Washington, D.C., and about to get a full-blown lesson on the most sordid part of our past. Was he too young?

It's common for African Americans to hear their first slavery stories—as Scotty did—when they are tots, fidgeting around a family table after a big meal, with several generations narrating, questioning and commenting in almost ritualistic fashion. It's an emotionally secure setting in which children can take in as much or as little as they can handle. They are surrounded by the warmth of kin, which softens the impact of fact.

That's a far cry from a kindergarten classroom. Scotty was fortunate that year to have a strong bond with his teacher, who remains a favorite. But Scotty was the only student in his class who both qualified to be called an African American and who readily identified himself as such. His classmates were mixtures or concentrates of Asians and Caucasians, African Americans and Latinos, European Americans and Central Americans.

So Scotty was alone in spirit when the class began a book written for children about the Underground Railroad. They pored over a picture of white men with shotguns and blood-hounds chasing black people—a young man and woman clutching a newborn as they fled through some woods—while the teacher read: "To be a slave meant that you had nothing you could call your own—not even your name."

Scotty came home preoccupied that day, and for many of the days that followed, he probed members of his large extended family about slavery. Mary Ann—who hadn't known beforehand that the class would dwell on the subject—went to see the teacher, who showed her a picture that had truly gripped Scotty. Even during "choice time," when he was free to play with anything, Scotty turned to this picture of a slave boy who had been savagely whipped before running away. The teacher then told of a discussion the children had after finishing the book. A white boy said to Scotty: "If we were alive back then, I would let you be free. I wouldn't make you work for me." Scotty was looking "a little uncomfortable" by then, the teacher said. He had brought the lesson to life. The class shrank from envisioning him in chains. And that was great for them, to get such a visceral sense of human bondage. But it cost Scotty considerably.

Mary Ann then felt compelled to show her son how the story ended. She took him to the rural part of Virginia where their ancestors had been enslaved, and where their relatives still live. She told him how their family started piecing together land before emancipation with pennies earned toiling for themselves after the master's work was done. She took him across the road to see the ruins of the mansion and told him how the white owners had to abandon the plantation after their vile slave-based economy fell apart. They couldn't make ends meet without our free labor, our strong spirits and our skills, she explained. Scotty listened soberly. Then they headed back across the road to the farm where his kin continue to thrive.

It's a risky business, knowing when and how to first reveal these dirty details of our history. Many African Americans cling to the old-timer's fear of traumatizing a child with too many specifics of the story. Elementary-school text books tend not to introduce slavery before third grade. However, more progressive educators, such as Beverly Gray, an African American expert on slavery studies from Chillicothe, Ohio, says that it's fine to expose children earlier as long as you do it in a secure setting.

"Kids need to be told the truth," Gray says. "They need to know how wrong it is to own another human being. It's also important to teach that we are survivors. . . and that we survived pretty much because we loved each other and we took care of each other, even those who weren't blood relations."

If you're not sure your child is ready emotionally to hear these truths, consult with his teacher. If she plans to teach slavery, perhaps your child can join another class during that period. Or you can stay on top of what he's taking in at school, so that you can augment the lessons at home, if need be. Just be sure you're not running from our history, because it's joint. We all have to own it.

19

Color Holidays, but Use All Shades of the Truth

If you're serious about sending your child out into the world free of unfounded biases against other peoples, you'll have work to do each time a holiday rolls around. For that's often when we seem to lose our sense of cultural balance. Imagine how differently you might feel about Thanksgiving, for instance, had you grown up hearing the story of the Pilgrims' first feast told by Native Americans. Consider telling your child an Indian tale of Thanksgiving such as this one, suggested by the Anti-Bias Curriculum Task Force:

> Suppose you lived in a house that you and your family loved very much. . . . One day some people came to your home from far away in big ships. They look very different from you, and at first you are afraid. Then, you remember your parents' teaching that all living things are your brothers. Your mom and dad invite these people into your beautiful home. These strangers have a long stick that kills your

brothers, the animals.... The Strange People make your family leave your home.... Every year after your family has left, the Strange People have a big party in your old house to celebrate taking it away from you.... They call their celebration Thanksgiving.

Now, we're not suggesting parents omit stories about our country's early European settlers and their hard-won triumphs over harsh winters and land they regarded as wild. We're asking you to think back to when you were a child and weigh the chances of your having formed a much different opinion of Indians—both as they struggled then, and today— had you known more about their perspective.

Rather than focusing on Thanksgiving's history, many Americans now use the day to express thanks for ways in which our personal or family lives have been graced. And that is fine. But if we're going to refer to the roots of Thanksgiving—or any other holiday—then we need to get the story straight, for our children's sake.

On Emancipation Day, for example, we praise Lincoln for freeing the slaves. Yet we conveniently forget that his proclamation only applied to slaves in the Confederate States, where it couldn't be enforced. Lincoln needed troops and hoped his edict would prompt slaves to desert their Southern masters and join forces with the North. Meanwhile, slaves in border states that were allied with the North remained in bondage.

On the Fourth of July, it somehow seems bad form to mention that one out of every five Americans was enslaved when our country declared independence from England, and that the bondage lasted nearly another century.

National holidays naturally appeal to our patriotism. For many, those are the only times we focus on our love of country. And we tend to go whole hog—even those of us who are still struggling for first class citizenship. We wallow in the sentiments that unite us until our eyes water and our vision is blurred, obscuring the ways we don't fit in with the mainstream. Then the flag-waving stops and we see that we're out there on our own, effectively jilted again.

America's many minorities and its bulge of "baby boomers" seem to be especially vulnerable to that emotional rollercoaster of raised and crushed expectations for our country. Perhaps that's because in our youth, we truly believed we could join forces and become a better people than we are today. Yet here we are as adults, in an America that seems to be saying our dreams are too expensive. And our democracy seems to be shrinking, rather than expanding.

Don't let America break your child's heart. Prepare him with the truth about our history—that it's marked by shame as well as glory. That way, he may be less likely to tune out or drop out, as previous generations have done when they discovered the thuggish strains of violence and greed that sometimes run as deeply and strongly in our country as do our most sacred ideals. Disillusion your child yourself, so he'll know there may never come a time when he won't have to be prepared to fight for what is right.

Teach your child to honor Old Glory, but also tell him about some of our country's double-dealings—involving Indians or Iranians, Vietnamese or our own veterans. The truth may be painful to hear, but it's a sign of our health that we know it to tell, and that we can voice it freely. Recast your holidays with all our nation's colors, and think of yourself as performing a patriotic act. Remind yourself and others that it's critical to our culture and our concept of justice that at least two sides of every story be told.

20

Avoid Cultural Tourism

Whoever came up with the idea that holidays are ideal times for children to learn about other cultures no doubt meant well. But as we've shown, holidays are tricky institutions. They may seem like conveniently located windows through which children can be directed to look and learn about other ways of life, but consider the view.

Holidays that focus on "other" people tend to trivialize them. They provide a safe margin of distance, across which cultural differences aren't threatening, but aren't quite real either. They present ethnicity as exoticism. They reduce culture to idiosyncrasies of song, food and dress.

As a result, our children may periodically pause to pay ceremonial tribute to other people, but they rarely get to know them. That makes our children mere tourists on the road to multiculturalism and means that we've taken a wrong turn in our efforts to broaden their horizons.

Many Native Americans, for example, despise the stereotypical image of "The Indian" that's dragged out for children's costumes each Thanksgiving and Halloween. Every nation did not look and dress like the Plains people, whose chief we see on cigar bands and football helmets, decked out in full war regalia, a bonnet of feathers framing his fiercely painted face.

Indeed, the title and role of "chief" both were imposed upon Native Americans by Europeans who were accustomed to the rule of monarchs. The tradition among many Indian nations previously had been for elders to take turns acting as head. It was an honorary, mostly ceremonial position. It was only during wartime that those nations were commanded by chiefs.

In fact, the Indians had such a representative and consensual means of governing themselves that some early-American scholars consider their system of councils to have been as much of an influence on the design of our federal system of democracy as the much-credited Magna Carta of England's oligarchy or the slave societies of ancient Greece. The word *caucus*, after all, comes from Algonquian, not from Latin.

So consider presenting Native Americans to your child as democratic pioneers rather than savage warriors. If they're saddled with a belligerent image today, it's mainly because European colonists consistently gave them good cause to fight. Cite the numbers. In 1500, around the time Columbus stumbled across America, there were more than 12 million Indians living in the present-day continental U.S. By the turn of the last century, there were less than a quarter of a million left. European settlers killed the Indians with their superior weaponry and their diseases. The settlers also "removed" entire nations of Indians from their homelands, pushing them westward on foot, at gunpoint, across the Mississippi along a "Trail of Tears."

Point out some of the ways we profited from Indians. Explain how most American cities are built on sites that were first selected and settled by Indians; that most of our highways and railroads trace Indian trails; that rather than forging paths through primeval forests or finding their way across vast, open plains, European pioneers simply followed Indians; that nearly half of the crops consumed around the world today were first domesticated by Native Americans; that the hardy, dependable potato, for example, freed Europe from periodic famine, enabling it to launch the Industrial Revolution.

During Black History Month, don't present slaves as helpless victims with no hope of escape until a big-hearted, powerful white person took pity on them. Try instead to emphasize the strength and faith and bravery of the captives, whose hands built much of our country and whose backs were its foundation.

The Underground Railroad is typically the first introduction to the history of Africans in America that young children get—largely because it is a popular topic among writers of children's books. Steer clear of ones in which all the conductors are sainted and white and the escaped slaves are little more than baggage on the train. Make sure your child knows that African Americans did more than sing during those days, as some of the books suggest. Many risked their all to work on the Underground. And there was a steady rain of rebellions and runaways as slaves sought to reclaim their freedom.

Be more than a tourist when it comes to other cultures. If you're just passing through, only lingering long enough to pick up some cheesy, stereotypical souvenirs, you might as well have stayed home.

21

Be Careful About What Your Children Read

Is the hero always white? If a black person plays a lead role in the story, does he succeed only because a white person comes riding to his rescue? Does a Latino triumph because he sees the errors of his culture's ways and abandons them in order to follow in an Anglo's footsteps? If these story lines sound familiar, then you have got the wrong books. You need to run—not walk—to the store or the library and get some new ones to read with your child.

For the first time ever, there's a fairly wonderful selection of books available featuring America's minorities. And many of them were written by minorities, in voices that are fresh and real. There also are many intriguing and enriching books on the market written by Third World authors about their countries of origin.

The scope of our children's curiosity is too often narrowed as they are bombarded by the media, the movies and the marketplace. Those commercial forces—along with peer pressure—determine what kids consider to be cool and what they will exclude.

Books are a means of opening up the world for children—magically transporting them to foreign lands or demystifying the lives that others lead closer by. They are maps for the world today and guides by which to plan tomorrow.

Of course, everything you and your child read should be chosen well. Here are a few trouble spots to avoid when evaluating books, taken from guidelines suggested by the Council on Interracial Books for Children:

- Flip through the book and check out the illustrations. Are hackneyed images used to portray minorities? Do the black people who are pictured always look happy-go-lucky? Does the Asian American seem inscrutable? Is the Chicano wearing a sombrero? Is the Native American naked, except for his loincloth? Are the Latinas either Madonna-like or loose? Do the pictures show people of many colors and ethnicities who all curiously have the same features—as if someone tinted them as an afterthought? Are the minorities always playing supporting, or passive, roles?

- Examine the storyline. Are the minority characters always the ones in trouble or with problems? If the minorities are poor and/or oppressed, does the story explain how they came to be so? Or does it lead the reader to assume that poverty is the minority's natural lot in life?

- If the book depicts the lifestyle of a minority family, does it do so mainly by comparing its "oddities" to the "normal" aspects of white middle-class America? Also be on the lookout for this tendency in books featuring natives of foreign countries and in books that focus on the cultural traditions that various immigrant Americans brought with them from the "old country."

- Does it seem like the hero merely happens to be black? When white America wants to champion a minority, it has a history of choosing an individual it doesn't feel culturally threatened by, that is, one who acts white.

- Consider the plot carefully to determine who the minority hero is fighting for—his people or white people or whatever other people. Optimally, of course, the hero should be fighting for the good of all people. But if he's not, if he's taking sides, make sure the moral of the story is one you choose to impart to your youngster.

- Who is the author? People tend to write from the perspective of their culture. Nearly all children's books, until very recently, were written by Eurocentric middle-class white people. Consequently, many of today's minority parents grew up mainly hearing stories about characters and settings that were foreign to their culture. Now that we have a wider choice of books and stories for our kids, we should make use of them. Children of all colors and cultures should regularly be encouraged to read stories about one another. Books make good introductions.

22

Think About How You Define Normal

Kai can't stop worrying about her son, seven-year-old Malik, and the rough time he has had getting settled in first grade. She's terrified when she thinks how casually a child can come so close to falling off track so early in life. She wonders whether to blame herself. Perhaps she unwittingly skipped something major in preparing her son for school. Kai, thirty-five, is raising Malik alone. She also works full-time and is taking courses toward a graduate degree, so she has had to cut a few corners. Malik is her first child and her only one. She would never claim to be an expert on motherhood. Even so, Kai says, her boy is no slacker, and he's not a troublemaker. He's bright and curious and charming, she beams. In fact, it could be that he's too charming for his. own good, Kai says, frowning now. He could simply be too much of an all-African-American boy for his teacher to take. Nothing's wrong with Malik's mind, the teacher tells Kai. But he won't sit still when he's supposed to, he doesn't pay enough attention, and he likes to clown around and entertain. Malik learns his lessons, but he's too active in class for his teacher's taste, which gets him in trouble, which makes him resentful, which Kai fears could put him on a permanent collision course with authority.

Black children—especially boys—are disproportionately tagged as disciplinary problems early on in their school careers. They are also prone to being misdiagnosed as having attention deficit disorders. The same traits that may be delightful to their loved ones often are troublesome to the school system. Lively little boys are spotted swiftly—often during their first week of grade school—and slapped with negative labels that sometimes stay with them for life. Furthermore, these stereotypical assessments appear to be made as often by teachers who are black, as Malik's is, as they are by whites.

The problem is largely due to teachers judging the demeanor and behavior of all children according to standards set by and for white children, says Janice E. Hale, an early-childhood education specialist at Wayne State University in Detroit. And what's "normal" for European Americans is not necessarily "normal" for African Americans.

For example, studies show a tendency for African babies to be more advanced in their motor development than European babies during the first year of life. It's unclear whether they are so by nature or because they're closer physically to their mothers, who often keep infants strapped to their bodies during much of the day. African American families also tend to be more emotionally expressive than European American ones, Hale says, and African American culture is highly dynamic.

In other words, African American households may well have more people and more generations present at any one time, who engage in a wider variety of interactions, often simultaneously, playing music while the television is on in the background, talking, and so on. When a child thrives on such levels of stimulation at home, he may find the monotony of school to be boring.

This topic is a thorny one and comes uncomfortably close to crude racial stereotypes. Anecdotal evidence of physical precocity among blacks has in the past been devalued by theories linking advanced motor development to lower mental ability and vice versa. Those theories have since been disproven. However there is clearly still a need for further study and comparison of the ways in which we develop and the patterns we present to our children as "normal." Mary Ann was repeatedly approached by parents of young black boys who were eager to talk about the nature of their sons' energy—how vibrant they find it to be. How magical—even theatrical—it often seems. How many ways in which it is simply *different*— when white boys are used as the standard for comparison.

When we looked at how many of the widely used psychological, behavioral and developmental measures *do* use white children as their base line, we began to listen more closely. Now we find ourselves agreeing with Hale, who argues that Americans are so set on becoming colorblind that we have become "culture-blind." Hale is challenging research institutions to fund more studies of the ways in which development proceeds normally for African American children and how culture and heritage affect their development, their school careers and, ultimately, their lives.

In the meantime, we should take better note of the many ways we use white people, their behavior and aspects of their cultures as absolute standards against which everyone else is to be measured, compared and defined. Is that a sensible or fair approach to life in our multicultural world? Observe your child's classroom to make sure that the standards considered normal there neither penalize nor benefit any one group. It can be just as harmful for a child to falsely believe he's better than others as it can be for a child to feel he's somehow worse.

23

Rule Out Discriminatory Remarks

On a Saturday afternoon in late October, Hodari was celebrating his eighth birthday with a large, boisterous party at a park near his grandmother's apartment building in suburban Maryland. The fare was nothing fancy: hot dogs cooked on a grill and an ice-cream cake.

It was a red-hot day that would be followed by a frosty evening—the time of year Hodari's grandmother grew up calling Indian summer. She shuns the term now, as she does most usages of the misnomer Columbus bestowed upon Native Americans 500 years ago. But she loves the season.

Parents sat around a picnic table while the group of kids— mostly boys from Hodari's very mixed public school class— ran freely and spiritedly around them. Every so often, a knot of boys would form and separate from the group. Shortly after that, a spat would develop. One of those times, as the boys engaged in a tugging war over a toy, some of them began to yell loudly at the others, accusing them of being Indian givers.

That's when Hodari's grandmother felt she had to intervene.

The boys seemed stunned to find the tall, stately African American woman with copper-brown skin and silver-gray hair towering above them. After all, none of their parents seemed bothered by their name-calling. As Hodari's grandmother made the boys see how hurtful she found the name to be, the boys insisted they meant no harm. Then she gave them a little history lesson, to show how misleading the epithet is. She told them about the U.S. government's record of breaking treaties it negotiated with Native Americans and then taking back the territory it had "given" the Indians to use.

The grandmother saw that two boys on the fringes of the group—one white and one black—were smirking and wise-cracking under their breath as she talked. "So whose feelings did we hurt?" one of them said. "Yeah, the Indians have been dead," said the other.

"Oh yeah?" Hodari piped up. "Then how come you're looking at one." His classmates were clearly surprised, having never thought of him being anything other than a black American. Their eyes shifted back to Hodari's grandmother, whose face seemed to look more Indian by the minute, as she told a simplified tale about the large numbers of escaped slaves and free African Americans who married into Native American nations.

It's said that so many blacks joined one particular nation that the Spaniards called them runaways—or "cimarrones," which evolved into their present-day name, Seminoles. Just goes to show that when you start calling names—especially in America, with all of its mixtures—you never know who you're insulting.

Hodari's grandmother is helping to raise him while her daughter juggles a full-time job and evening classes at a community college. She says she has been disturbed lately by the lack of importance the parents of Hodari's friends seem to attach to ethnic slurs, cultural slights and derogatory remarks made about various physical traits that define the races.

They don't seem as alert to the inflammatory dangers of discriminatory remarks as her generation was, she says. Rather than criticize, parents tend to ignore a child who resorts to such insults. They act as if the behavior will cease if no attention is called to it. Instead, they are essentially granting their children permission to behave in discriminatory ways.

Some parents try to excuse their children's behavior, claiming they didn't mean to be offensive or that they didn't grasp the gravity of their words. If children don't understand these things, it's because parents haven't made them clear.

Other parents downplay the importance of their child's discriminatory words or actions—especially if there is no immediate or obvious reaction on the part of the person who was targeted. ("See, no harm was done!")

Tell your child early and often that there is no excuse for racist remarks or discriminatory behavior. Don't ignore them; don't excuse them; don't try to rationalize them away. They are simply wrong.

The Upper Elementary School Years

Ages nine to eleven could be dubbed "The Awakening Years"— though at times the awakening is a rude one. This is both a glorious and scary stage as the child gradually becomes aware of who he is and what he *wants* to stand for. There is a great deal of change between the ages of nine and eleven, the start and finish of prepuberty, but generally, these growing children are able to distinguish their own inner values and attitudes from those of their peer group. For example, their friends may want them to talk endlessly on the phone, but they have a nagging voice inside that says, "I need to get off the phone if I want to finish my homework."

Our society doesn't concern itself with children of this age as much as it does those in preadolescence and adolescence. And yet, these years are crucial. They require the parent's full attention as the child wavers between falling back on his parents and striving for independence.

As for signs of prejudice, they are there, but nine- to ten-year-olds are more caught up in their physical or mental shortcomings than in the differences of their skin color. A typical complaint might be, "Peter got mad at me because I'm so slow. I'll never be fast." Nevertheless, a parent's response to this kind of statement can set the stage for the child's attitude toward people of other races and cultures. Parents who help their child through his uncertainty by building his self-esteem and self-confidence are paving the way for his adult inclination to respect himself and others. Children at this age are particularly eager to do things with their parents and family. In fact, they will admire and boast about their parents, siblings and extended family. Experts tell us that this is an especially ripe time for parents to enjoy the company of their children of the same sex. Through shared activities—shopping, bike riding, going to baseball games—mothers and daughters, fathers and sons, form a bond that enhances the development of the child and makes life all the more precious.

What makes this bonding so easy is the nine- to eleven-year-old's insatiable appetite for exploring and hands-on activities. They don't just want to hear about the Civil War; they want to drive to the battlefield and run around the hills. They want to make elaborate experiments for their science project. Animals, insects, computers, sports, all fascinate and consume them with a passion you've never seen before. This is a wonderful time for parent and child to explore new worlds together. One African American mother recalls how as a child she always hated to go to art galleries because none of the paintings depicted black people. Now, she makes a point to take her ten-year-old daughter to concerts, art shows and theater events that feature work from both white and black communities.

Not all is bliss at this time, especially around the eleven-year mark. Prepuberty generally means rapid body changes, leaving the child feeling like he is either lagging behind or zooming ahead of his friends. The developing child becomes fixated on parts of his body that he may vehemently claim to hate, such as his nose, complexion or legs. He may suffer mood swings and become his own worst judge, especially when he is dealing with his peers. If a friend makes an unkind remark—which kids at this age seem to do routinely—he is devastated and reacts negatively, blaming himself rather than the friend or the circumstance.

Up to age eleven is an intense time for kids to juggle what is right and wrong. They are bowled over by what is unfair in the classroom or what they see on TV and on the news. Even though they are very capable of breaking the rules, they are well-versed in what the rules are, often upholding them in order to receive praise and approval from their parents.

Eleven-year-olds, however, are not always as co-operative and rule abiding; they don't always idealize or favor mother and father, as they did just a year before. They talk back, withdraw, don't do their chores. They suddenly look around and decide that other people are different, or a problem, and they're not sure they want to be affiliated with people not like them. It is a sensitive and decisive time, which calls for a parent's patience, support and guidance.

24

Insist on Respect

A fifth grade boy complains to his mother, "All they ever talk about at school is respect, respect." And yet when things go awry, his mother says, "My son is quick to notice and declare self-righteously that 'The coach wasn't fair to my friend,' or that 'Karen was mean to me.' He actually wants people to respect one another, just as he wants others to respect him."

With your child being so alert to what is fair and unfair, now is an opportune time for you to state clearly that you expect him to have a courteous regard for others, both at home and outside of the family, regardless of the other's race or creed.

Set limits to the style and content of criticism, especially of siblings and friends: "You can be angry with your sister, but you don't scream in her face or touch her in your anger. You respect her as an individual, and you listen to her side of the story."

Tell your child that respect means acknowledging that everyone has rights and needs. This means all people, all races. Insist on respect for the family unit: Teach him to stay at the dinner table until everyone has finished; to say thank you and pardon me; to knock on bedroom doors before entering. Explain to your child that you are not enforcing good manners just for the sake of it. There are reasons behind manners—they communicate respect for other people.

When out shopping or doing errands, if he should make fun of the way a person is dressed or looks, teach him not to judge others by the ways in which they are different from him. Don't just scold him or shame him; talk it through by asking him why he thinks that person "looks that way" and how he would feel if someone were to make fun of the way he dressed or looked.

When watching the news, or talking about the school day, you can use relevant incidents to point out how difficult it is when people no longer respect one another. What you are doing is raising his sensitivity to unfairness.

Do the same sensitivity training when it comes to positive incidents of fairness. Point out to your child how beneficial it is when he or his teacher or your neighbor considers someone else's feelings.

Try to refrain from making your lessons on respect too personal. Instead, engage your child in open-ended questioning using hypothetical situations: "What would you do if you were told you couldn't participate in a game because you have a different skin color?" "What would happen if you were Latino and someone called you lazy? How would you feel? How would you react?" This game of generalized questions allows your child to be less defensive, and it should lead to a thoughtful discussion.

Emphasize that you aren't expecting your child to like everyone, but you are expecting him to show respect.

A white mother with two adopted black children says,

"You don't force your child to go out into a situation and then say, 'You have to like all those kids on that team, or all those kids in that class.' But you do absolutely have to teach them to respect who they are. I think sometimes we get that mixed up, that liking and respecting thing."

A common frustration among parents today is the feeling that they can teach their kids respect, but it doesn't do much good when there are so many other children who haven't been taught the same kindness or rules, particularly toward children of other races or toward children unlike themselves.

What would happen, however, if you lowered your expectations of your child and allowed him to be disrespectful, like some of the other children in his class or neighborhood? Undoubtedly, the problem would grow worse for all concerned. The answer can only be that you have to stick with it and teach the rules of respect. Every effort on your part will be of value to your child now and on into adulthood.

25

Nurture and Spread Self-Esteem

Even though this is a joyous age, it has its rocky times. A child's self-esteem plummets with the most incidental remark from a friend or a disapproving glance from a teacher. It is also a time when the child can feel wonderful about himself but needs to be reassured often that he's as great as he thinks he is, or would like to be.

Most parents know that it's important to boost and nurture their child's self-esteem. They may need to be reminded, however, that a healthy self-esteem has an equally healthy ripple effect on society. Five eleven-year-olds met with Barbara on a school night to talk about the race issues they face with their friends and in sports. Three of the children were black, one was white, and one identified himself as having a white mother and a black father. All of the children demonstrated a strength in knowing who they are and wanting to be fair to others. When the white boy talked about the time the black kids didn't select him for a pickup game of basketball, his voice cracked, and he couldn't finish the story. His black friend came to the rescue: "But then you went back and subbed and showed 'em you're good, didn't ya? That's all you got to do; show 'em you're good!"

That's what parents have to do. Show your child his or her own goodness.

- Articulate and affirm how you accept her for who she is rather than trying to change her personality. If your child is feisty, shy, serious or compulsive, whatever the trait may be, accept that trait as hers and as worthwhile.

- Be there for her and listen to her problems and worries. Dr. Stanley Greenspan points out that it's hard for parents not to jump in with advice, especially when they think a child is not acting up to their expectations. At this age, he says, it is important for the parent not to offer quick solutions but rather to spend time with their child and recognize her need to talk through her problems.

- Acknowledge her dreams and pursuits even when you think they are unreasonable or unattainable. She wants to be a doctor or a professional athlete? Fine. She wants to be popular and smart? Great. Nothing should stand in her way, especially not the color of her skin or her cultural background.

- Give her a sense of pride in her race. Present your race and culture in a positive and admirable way. Point out leaders or public figures who voice your thoughts and opinions on race. Do the same with others within your family and community. A child's pride in her grandparents is enhanced when she understands the context of their struggle; describe what they achieved despite the burden of prejudice.

- Tell her you love her, and let her know that as far as you are able, you'll be there for her whenever she has problems.

Marco is a bright, talented eleven-year-old from Colombia, in South America, whose white adoptive parents have always supported him and his love of music. He would rather play the piano than shoot baskets at the neighborhood recreation center in Queens, New York, where all the boys gather after school and during weekends. On several occasions these boys have called Marco "nigger," and one particular eleven-year-old boy taunted him: "Go back to Colombia. Your white parents aren't your real parents. They don't love you."

While all this is sad and difficult, with the support and guidance of his parents, Marco has been able to rise above it and make plans to go to a magnet school for the arts. "He knows he is very special," says his mother.

Healthy self-esteem is crucial in this world. A child needs to hear that she is valuable and special. By instilling in her a strong sense of self-respect, she will be better equipped and more resourceful in facing the segments of society that abuse or ignore her race and culture. She will also be more sensitive to others and their needs, valuing them as she values herself.

26

Know Your Child's Role Models

If you want to keep track of the crucial role models in your child's life, you have to make a concentrated effort to know your child's teachers, coaches, counselors and school principal. Through their example and formal instruction, your child is learning how to respect people of all races and backgrounds. Or is he? You need to know whether these role models are delivering the message of fairness that you want your child to hear.

Don't depend on hearsay from your friends and neighbors. Everyone may tell you that the fifth grade teacher is biased, but you have to decide for yourself, and that can be done only by introducing yourself and observing his classroom style. Whatever you do, don't depend on your child's description as the final word. You should listen to your child's opinion because he may be very accurate in his assessment of a prejudiced instructor. But you still need to meet with the teacher and come to your own conclusions.

Here are some tips gathered from various schools around the country. They can apply to all teachers, whether they teach science, piano or soccer.

Visit your child's teacher before there are any problems. Don't plan the visit on the first back-to-school night when there are dozens of other parents talking to the teacher; it's best to make an appointment a few weeks after school has started and the teacher is familiar with your child.

If possible, observe the teacher at work with the class. Does he fairly call on all students, or does he play favorites based on race, gender or performance?

The same holds true for coaches. Go to the games or practices; listen to the way the kids are spoken to. Competition is the essence of sports; but does the coach inappropriately compare kids to one another by using racial slurs? One parent heard a coach cry out in a fury, "You're playing like a lazy Spic!" Even though there were no Spanish-speaking kids on the team, the offensive remark used by such an authority figure would be likely to influence any child's attitudes. In this incident, the parent failed to intervene, thereby missing an opportunity to teach both coach and child a lesson.

If you have to cancel and reschedule your appointment at school, do it yourself. Don't make your child the messenger. Teachers complain that parents assume wrongly that teachers are always there after school and aren't inconvenienced by last-minute cancellations or by a parent showing up unannounced. What does such etiquette have to do with racism? If you want to keep a good working relationship with your child's teacher, you have to respect his life. It helps keep the doors open for communication.

If you can't visit, write notes or call. This is especially important if there are problems brewing. Let the teacher know that you are aware of the situation and that you want to be kept informed.

If there are racial issues between your child and his peers, or with the teacher, discuss them openly and honestly. Ask questions; ask the teacher for his view. If you don't like what you hear, and you fear your child may be singled out for reprisals, consider joining forces with other parents who have similar complaints—this will take time and effort, but it may give you a stronger case. Next, go to the principal and ask him to preside over a meeting of parents and the teacher.

Give the solution time to take hold. But if you don't get results, don't hesitate to go to the top. A Latina mother was disturbed by reports from her son that his day camp counselor refused to call him by his name, Ricardo. "He would only call him 'Richard,'" she said, "even though my son asked him several times not to." Each day the mother wrote notes to the counselor, to no avail. Finally, she went to see the camp director, and the problem was remedied within the day.

Uninformed parents can overreact to what a child tells them about a teacher. Many teachers say that they are intimidated, even attacked, by parents who storm into the school declaring them biased or racist. In most of these incidents, the teachers had never met the parents before the problems had exploded. Such scenes wouldn't happen as frequently if, early in the school year, more parents would get to know their child's teachers and establish a respectful rapport. Let teachers know that you expect them to be role models of fairness for your child, and that you are grateful for their example.

27

Help Broaden Your Child's Social Circle

It's Friday night. You want to order a pizza and get a video so you can collapse in a mindless state on the couch, but your daughter wants to invite two friends to a sleep-over. "Which two friends?" you ask, coming out of your haze. Linda and Jen, her two best friends. Okay, you agree half-heartedly, and then you come up with the daring idea: Why not ask Mary too? She might like to come, and it would be nice to get to know her.

This wonderful stage, between the ages of nine and eleven, is probably the last time a parent can have a strong influence on the child's choice of peers. Use this opportunity to encourage your child to develop diverse friendships, and to respect children of all colors.

As mothers, Barbara and Mary Ann well know that this takes planning and sheer energy, but once it becomes part of your routine, it will enhance your child's life.

- Let your child know that her friends are always welcome in your home—when you are there. Don't rely on your child to come up with activities to do with a friend. More than likely, you will have to help with the planning. It doesn't have to be elaborate or cost money—they can ride bikes, watch television or make dessert for dinner.

- Respect their right to privacy and give them space to work out their friendship, but don't be a stranger; engage the children in conversation when it is appropriate. One mother notes that she rarely sits down with her son and his friends—if she did, they would stop talking immediately. Instead, as they eat, she works nearby in the kitchen, and they chat casually with her.

- Do chores with your child and her friend. Wash the car, rake leaves, walk the dog. All the while, talk about school or what interests them most, such as movies, sports or computer games. As you do this, listen to how your child and her friend regard each other. If it is with respect, occasionally praise them for that (don't gush or overdo it), or praise your child later when you are alone.

- If you feel your child is being disrespectful to her friend, call it to her attention when it is appropriate. For instance, if it is a borderline slight, you may choose to wait until you are alone; if it is very offensive, you should bring it up immediately.

- Help your child develop multicultural friendships by suggesting activities that include other children from her class or neighborhood. Don't invite a child over just because she belongs to another race, but do show your child that people shouldn't be excluded simply because they look different. A white mother of an adopted Korean child often plans sleep-overs with various boys from her son's fourth grade. "It's exhausting," she says, "but this way my son can be with his two Asian friends who are so important to him, as well as with others."

- Be careful that you don't project your own prejudice and anxiety by holding back from inviting children of other races to your home. Mary Stewart Bargar, a teacher in New Haven, Connecticut, whose classes have a majority of blacks and a minority of whites and Hispanics, says: "Often the kids want to socialize, but the parents are reluctant to invite them over." Bargar suggests to these parents that they arrange for their children to meet and play in public places, such as the park or playgrounds, after school and on weekends. Somehow the neutral ground enables the parents to break through their barriers of prejudice and allows their children to play together. Though not an ideal situation, it is a start.

- Make an effort to know the parents of your child's friends as well. Barger points out that this makes the logistics— driving children and setting up times to play—much easier. It also demonstrates to your child that you are interested in getting to know her friend's family.

All this takes dedication and savvy, but by being an involved parent, you can make sure that your child socializes with respect, and you can challenge her to broaden her friendships with others.

28

Expose Racial Stereotyping in Entertainment

Rich whites, dumb blacks, lazy Latinos, nerdy Asians. Welcome to the world of television, the strongest perpetrator of racial stereotyping. From sitcoms to rap music on MTV to the evening news, kids are saturated with messages that depict minorities as insolent, foolish and violent, and whites as well-off, canny if not smart, and law-abiding. Few parents can control what their child watches or listens to; the only way for a parent to combat the powerful and intrusive influence of the entertainment world and the television media is to jump in and become part of it.

- Watch your child's favorite shows along with her. Once you determine that a show is realistic, or harmless, you don't have to watch it together every week, but keep in touch with evolving episodes and characters.

- Be alert to all racial stereotyping on shows, including car- toons. Point them out to your child as they appear on the screen.

- Include news shows in your monitoring. Numerous minority parents testify that their children are annoyed by how the "bad guys" on the news are always black or Hispanic. "Why are they always the ones with handcuffs on?" says one boy to his father. When blacks or other minorities are covered in "good" news or recognized for their community involvement, make sure that your child notices.

- Prepare yourself for your child's protests: "Oh Mom, you're always interrupting" or "Don't take it so seriously, Dad." Nonetheless, stick to your message about stereo- types and misrepresentations of races and cultures. Eventually, it will sink in.

- Watch MTV at night, without your child, to get an idea of what he is tuning in to. Try to listen to the words to rap songs on the radio or MTV. Later, ask your child as you listen together, "What are they saying?" and "What does that mean?" A mother of four children makes a wise observation: "When you come in the room and ask ques- tions about the music, if they squirm or turn off the TV or radio, they're feeling embarrassed or guilty. But that's all right, they're supposed to feel that! When they aren't responding, parents should worry."

- Introduce your child to quality shows that depict a cast that is multicultural or racially varied. To find them, read descriptions of shows listed in your newspaper or televi- sion guide. This will also protect you from surprises in plot lines.

Fred Cooke is an African American father of four children and a communications attorney. It's a job, he says, that makes him particularly sensitive to the misrepresentation of blacks on television. When his nine-year-old and eleven-year-old are watching a sitcom that shows the black character as idiotic, Cooke deliberately "bugs" his children with questions: "Do you know anyone like that in our family?" and "Do you know anybody who acts that way?"

"All of this is driven by images in the heads of white producers and decision makers," says Cooke. "And it's based on what they think black people want to see. This is what white people think black people are. It doesn't make sense, but it continues."

The best way to lick the racist material on television and in music is to familiarize yourself with it and help your child question it. Much as you would like to, don't walk away or tune it out. It's too much a part of your child's world.

The Young Teen Years

The early teens, which for some start as young as eleven, are often marked by turmoil and uncertainty, as childhood slips away and adulthood looms ahead. Parents need to remember that it is normal for their young teen to be ambivalent, rebellious, bored, disinterested or just plain difficult to be around. "Whatever happened to my child?" laments many a parent of a young teen. Suddenly and dramatically, these growing children are showing signs of prejudice and elitism. They are highly critical of others who don't look or act like them, and they do all they can to identify with a pre-ferred group of friends, in the way that they dress, talk or select the music they listen to. It's maddening as these teens either ignore their parents or speak in mumbled monosyllables. Meanwhile, they have no problem conversing with each other—in a language all their own.

Underneath this turmoil is a child who continues to need love. It's okay to hug a thirteen-year-old, even if he acts embarrassed about your open affection. It's smart and important to meet your fourteen-year-old's friends, even if she says she doesn't want to invite them over. Despite their coolness, young teens need to know that their parents are concerned about them and their welfare.

These teens now view rules and morality as things that are imposed on them by their parents, not as ways for society to keep order or to keep people from getting hurt. (Be patient—the under-standing of morality will come during the older adolescent years.) Young teens tend to make moral choices according to what pleases their peers, not their parents. This may explain why even the very best behaved children break rules about staying out late, or why they experiment with racial stereotyping and racial harassment.

Young adolescence is distinctively marked by the need to belong to a group. This doesn't necessarily mean that young teens focus on one-on-one friendships, or that they all want to be very popular or the leader of a pack. It simply means that they want to identify with and be accepted by a particular group of kids. It may be three kids who excel in the science lab, or it may be the entire soccer team; whatever the size or identity, it is a group that defines "cool" as a person who is one of them. Experts say that belonging to a group is part of developing an identity, and parents shouldn't dismiss how important it is to the teen. Dr. Haim Ginott, an authority on child development, challenges this idea by telling parents that they "should let their teen know that they value integrity over popularity." That may be easier to do in the later teen years, when autonomy is more valued than peer pressure. Still, parents should let their child know that when they exclude others from the group, or defame others, it goes against a basic family and societal value—respect.

Perhaps the hardest task for parents is to allow their young teen to go his own way and to experiment with new ideas. Parents who insist that their child conform to what they believe are only asking for trouble further down the road. This holds true for any kind of heavily applied pressure, from insisting on strict religious observance to enforcing nonracist behavior. Parents need to make it clear to their teen what their views are and to allow him to express his own views. By doing so, parents are not only legitimizing their teen's world, they are also helping him become more independent. Child development experts reassure parents that young teens may have values that differ from those taught in the home, but that later, as young adults, they often return to their parents' basic beliefs.

29

Select a Diverse Middle School

Many of the teens Barbara spoke to drew a correlation between their unbiased views and the degree of *healthy* diversity in the schools that their parents had chosen for them. "If they had sent me to a private, all-white school, I'd probably feel very differently," says a white teen who believes that attending a highly diverse school as he does, is a bonus.

We are all products of our environment, and if that environment has been a homogenous, isolated one, we are ill-prepared to face diverse and complex situations. If parents—especially white ones—want their child not only to survive but to thrive in a multicultural world, they have to provide a multicultural education and environment.

We're not suggesting that you suddenly change where your children go to school. What we are asking is that when the time comes for choices, which is often at the middle-school level, you look beyond your culture and comfort zone and expose your child to a multicultural education, especially if he has been attending a grade school with little or no diversity.

Don't rely on neighborhood hearsay to make your decision. Call the schools you are considering, and ask for the current breakdown of the student body by race.

Arrange with the school office to attend an all-school event, such as an assembly, so you can observe the school in session. This may be better than picking a class at random and seeing only a tiny portion of the school in action.

Meet with the school counselor or principal or vice principal, and ask how the school goes about encouraging multiculturalism. Do they offer workshops on diversity or teach problem-solving techniques? Is the staff multicultural? Inquire whether they teach multicultural history and literature throughout the school year, or for only a month, or a day.

Get a copy of the school newspaper, and read about the school in your local newspaper—get a feel for what the kids are interested in and how much cultural interaction exists.

If possible, ask the opinion of older teens who have graduated from the school. Often, they can offer a perspective that you won't find in print or statistics.

Not all parents have the luxury or opportunity to pick a middle school for their young teen. But those who do should try to find a school that exposes their child to the realities of a multicultural world and teaches them the skills to survive in it.

30

Listen To and Discuss Your Teen's Concerns

A group of ninth graders—two whites and four blacks—who have known one another since grade school, gathered to talk about racial conditions in their school, which draws from neighborhoods of varying income levels throughout their city. Eventually, the conversation turned to the violence among some of the girls in the school. Not wanting to disclose any names, they described a physical fight that took place between two girls—one black and one Hispanic—who scratched each other's faces and pulled hair. The students weren't sure what caused this particular fight. They just knew there had been trouble between these two girls, who were known to exchange racial slurs and to compete for the same boys. Such fighting isn't all that unusual, these ninth graders said, though they neither take part in nor approve of it. When asked what their parents thought of the fighting, one of the black girls shrugged her shoulders and said, "They don't know. We don't want to worry them."

No matter how close your relationship, don't expect your young teens to come to you directly when there are major issues in their lives, such as discrimination among their peers or violence in the school.

Parents need to initiate conversations, as well as ask questions. Go beyond the usual "How was your day?" because you're bound to get the proverbial sigh and answer, "Fine." Pose questions that don't solicit a one-word response: "What happened in assembly today?" "Tell me about your new science teacher; what is she like?"

Persevere. If your teen doesn't want to talk today, try again tomorrow or two days later. This is a time when they feel pressured by your interest, and they have to make sure you aren't judging them or smothering them with concern.

Finding the time to talk and listen can be a problem. The most common complaint of parents today is that their lives are "too busy." Unfortunately, that means we don't have enough time to be with and talk to our children. Long working hours and a host of after-school activities make family dinner hours nearly obsolete. For parents who are divorced or separated, conversations with their children are weighed down by complicated custody scheduling and family politics. A middle-school counselor, who calls on her background as the mother of a thirteen-year-old boy, advises today's parents to "capture" every moment you have with your child, no matter how frantic the moment might be. "Talk to your kid whenever you can. Do it while he's in the car and you're driving on errands. Do it while you're doing chores together on the weekends. Just talk."

Don't assume that because there is no discussion, there is no problem.

One black fourteen-year-old girl says that her mother apparently never notices that she socializes with fewer blacks than whites. "She wouldn't like that if she knew, but she never asks me about it, so it's not an issue," says this teen, with a look that defies her bravado.

If you're having trouble engaging your child in conversation, bring in your own experiences as a young teen by being sympathetic or curious: "When I went to school, I had no experience with friends from another race. What's it like for you?" When you try this, don't overload him with recollections. Focusing too much on your own ancient history will ignite your teen's red light, cutting off the dialogue. Again, give time for him to absorb what you are saying. Even if he doesn't start talking then, he may bring it up later.

If you want to keep the communication lines open with your teen, don't overreact to what he tells you. A white mother was casually talking to her son about what was happening in their neighborhood, which consists of whites, blacks and Hispanics. She was shocked to learn that he and a group of his white friends have been dubbed "wiggers," meaning that they are whites who hang out with blacks. Though it infuriated her, she calmed down enough to say that this was a slur and an unfortunate one. Instead of saying (as she wanted to), "That's horrible, absolutely horrible!" she asked him: "Does being called that make any difference when you're deciding who your friends are?" Her son said, no, he would still have black friends, but that the name still made him feel awful. "At least I was able to tell him I was proud of how he was handling it," she said later. When she reported this story at a small gathering of middle-school parents, several of the black mothers expressed their surprise and concern for what she and her son were going through. They told her that they had never heard the term *wigger*. "Tell your son to be strong," said one black mother. "I know your boy well; he's a good kid."

Parents have to take the time to talk and listen to their

teen's concerns. This means concentrated effort and dedication, which don't come easily in our busy lives. Let your teen know he is not alone in coping with frightening and challenging issues. You can't always solve his problems, but you can listen.

31

Don't Use Racism as a Crutch

At a conflict resolution meeting held during the school lunch hour, a ninth grader complained to a dozen other students and the faculty advisor that her English teacher was "a racist" because he didn't call on her in class. "I know it's because I'm black," she said adamantly. However, another ninth grader, a white girl, then pointed out that she had the same teacher the preceding semester and he also treated her with indifference. "I think he's a bad teacher and has favorites," she said. "There are a lot of black boys that he does call on."

Be careful that your teen doesn't automatically blame racism for her problems in school. Both you and your child should consider the bigger picture and learn to recognize when other, perhaps equally offensive, factors are at work— such as sexism. And don't rule out the possibility that your own actions can sometimes trigger distasteful results that have nothing to do with racism.

This is a sensitive and unresolved topic among parents, teens and teachers alike, across the racial spectrum. Where do you draw the line between what is racism and what is not?

There's an example often given: A black or Hispanic teenager insists that a teacher is discriminating against her by giving her a lower grade or treating her differently than the whites in the class. What should the parent do?

First, assure your child that you share her concern. Second, look at the evidence; look at her work. Has she completed her assignments, answered questions correctly, read the books she was supposed to read? Use your own good judgment, and try to be as objective as a parent can possibly be. If you can't discern what the problem is, ask for a teacher conference, and arrange to observe the class. Watch closely how the teacher treats other students.

If you determine that your child is being treated unfairly, meet with the teacher as soon as possible, and present all your evidence. Screaming "racist" probably won't help. Bring the principal and/or a school counselor into the picture, and offer evidence of your claim, particularly if you don't see any hope for a resolution by dealing with the teacher alone.

If you decide that your child is getting the grade she deserves, make it clear to her that racism is not the culprit this time, and it is her responsibility to do better.

Mary Estes Henry, a black educator and former middle-school counselor, is a strong believer in personal accountability. "I don't believe in talking to kids and letting them make excuses. I tell kids, 'You've got to go ahead, do your best, develop skills.'

"I think parents have to encourage kids to learn, get involved in activities, get to know teachers in school and not let race serve as a crutch for every little mishap," says Henry. "When I hear kids say, 'I should have gotten an A, but I got a B,' I tell them, 'Just keep striving. You're always going to have pitfalls. If you can't go over the mountain, go around it or through it.'"

32

If Trouble's Brewing, Sound the Horn

A woman overheard her son talking about a student carrying a weapon into school. For weeks there had been rumors of a white gang that was harassing the few black kids who attend their private school. The school administration had difficulties identifying the gang members. There were no visible clues, such as gang jackets or shirts—this was a school where everyone was required to wear a uniform. Also, none of the students would come forward and name who was involved. So in spite of her child's protests, this mother didn't hesitate to call the principal and report who was carrying a weapon. The student was apprehended, and the parents and principal were greatly relieved that they were able to stop what could have turned into a nasty incident, or even a loss of life.

When you get a whiff of racial tension, or a possible racial encounter in your child's school, blow the whistle by alerting the school authorities. Be confident that your involvement will make a difference. Call or go to the school, or when it is not a matter of life and death, write notes to the teacher and principal in which you make clear the problems and how you suggest they be remedied.

Form a parents' network—through the parent-school organization, your friends in the school or your neighborhood. Use the telephone to keep one another abreast of developments; appoint one or two parents to communicate with the school when necessary. Again, be clear in describing the problem and what you want done about it. If you are ambivalent, chances are you will be ignored. The principal at a private boys' school claims that it has been able to curb racism solely through the efforts of the parents, who formed a strong telephone network.

Some parents don't get involved because they don't want to implicate their child, or because their child insists that they "don't interfere." There's no doubt that your teen is your worst critic—he doesn't want you to do anything that would embarrass him or make him look as though he is ratting on his peers. In some cases, he's not convinced of the seriousness of the problem. Nevertheless, don't hide your whistle-blowing—always let your child know what you are doing. Expect some argument, but stick to your convictions.

Realize that teachers and principals welcome your information and concern. "Society expects schools to create miracles with their kids," says a Hispanic teacher who copes with racial division everyday in her classroom. "We can't do it all. We need the parents' help."

33

Learn Compassion for All Colors

It was a Friday night, a time when most kids are scrambling to find some action. Sixty students representing three public schools and two private schools found theirs in a four-hour diversity training workshop held in the cavernous library of a Washington, D.C., public school. Boys and girls, Christians, Jews, Muslims, Asians, Latinos, Hispanics, blacks, whites and a small group of parents approached the student-led exercises cautiously. By the evening's end, however, many had voiced heartfelt concerns, and more than a few had shed tears.

During the training, everyone was encouraged to express their negative and positive perceptions of their own race, as well as others. "I don't like Latino men because they don't take responsibility," said one teen, during an exercise where he is allowed to say whatever bad feelings come to mind about his own people. Minutes later, during another exercise in which he's meant to express pride about his race, he smiles and says: "I like Latino men because they come to this country and beat all odds." This isn't a contradiction, explained one of the workshop leaders. This is life; there are people who succeed and people who mess up. And just as important, many of us have a love/hate relationship with our origins.

In this particular method of diversity training, by exposing their personal experiences with prejudice—whether over race, religion, gender, sexuality or class—the students develop their sensitivity and compassion, as they realize that at one time or another they all have been victims of blind and cruel judgments. By the end of this workshop, many of the students said that from now on, they would be willing to speak out whenever they hear prejudice among family and friends; they also said they wanted to help people understand the origins of their prejudice. And yet, one of the teenage leaders warned them: "Don't expect miracles. It takes a long time to get to the point where other people will listen to you. But this is a start."

Diversity sensitivity training is a tangible tool for fighting racism. There are many different methods of training available. Call your school counselor or principal and suggest that your school hire a diversity expert (or consulting firm) to hold workshops for teachers. If your school is not familiar with such resources, call the state offices of your parent-school organization, and they should be able to give you referrals.

To save on cost and time, the teachers and the counselors at the school who have completed the instruction can go on to train teenage students and parents, who can then go on to train other students and parents.

Once you have a small core of trained teachers and students, the workshop can be part of the school curriculum. Many schools conduct their workshops during two consecutive English classes, so that all students eventually receive the training. Depending on the size of your school, it may take several months before the entire school body has received training.

It's important to have parents involved; workshops don't

have to place parents and teens together, but parents should at least be informed. If parents can't attend the workshops, send them a written description of the program and its methods.

During a sensitivity workshop's "speak out" exercise, where students say what angers them most, an African American boy talked about his concern for his younger sister, whom he believed would face discrimination from other black people because of her light skin. "I worry about her," he said, despondently. "She is too sweet to stand up to their criticism." Another student angrily described how teachers and adults marveled over the fact that she had gotten into a top college. She said, "They think that it's exceptional because I'm black!" And a white student spoke out in exasperation: "Just because I'm white, and a man, don't assume I'm racist."

At the start of the sensitivity workshop held on Friday night, the principal told the students, "Your differences are both your strength and your Achilles' heel. By the end of the workshop you will be accepting and appreciating other people and their differences."

34

Encourage Community Service

Dana has chocolate smeared up to her elbows. For two hours she has been cutting frozen chocolate cakes and wrapping the sticky pieces in small plastic bags. It's a dreary, rainy Saturday, and this fourteen-year-old is working with a crew of volunteers at Martha's Table, a shelter in Washington, D.C., that feeds hundreds of homeless each day. "If I didn't have to be here," says Dana with a wide grin, "I'd be in my bed—asleep!"

Dana, like a growing number of teenagers, is doing community service as part of her school curriculum. When she completes twenty hours of volunteering at participating charitable organizations, her work will go toward her religious studies grade. It's a system that satisfies all concerned—the charitable agency, the school and especially the students. "I love doing my service," says Dana. "Everywhere I go, the people are so nice. But I really like the job of answering phones," she adds, frowning at the sticky mess of chocolate.

Adolescence is an age that rises to the call for help. From feeding the poor to teaching the illiterate, the young are sensitive to the ills born of society's neglect. This is a time for parents to encourage and respect their teenagers for serving the community. No matter how simple the task, distributing blankets, answering phones or tending to the sick—the volunteer teen is helping to bridge racial and cultural divisions with her concern and acts of kindness for other human beings.

Child development experts confirm what common sense tells us: Community service not only makes a child feel good, she also gains a sense of importance, and a sense of community. Barbara adds that when a teenager works alongside volunteers from other races, everyone gains. For example, Dana, who is black, worked at the shelter with two whites and another black—a college student and two working women—all cutting chocolate cakes while talking, laughing and sharing stories about their families and life. At that work table, there was a viable sense of community and no space for racial tension.

- You can easily find places for your child to volunteer through public listings in your local newspaper, at the public library's bulletin board and through your place of worship. Check with your middle school's or high school's counseling department, which usually oversees community service programs that are part of the curriculum in a growing number of schools.

- Do your own community service. Your example will not only be an inspiration to your child but also a way to see how such commitment takes planning, hard work and dedication. An African American mother says she grew up in a Baptist home that boasted the motto: "Instead of just talking, our family takes action." For years she has been a mentor to children in housing projects. Now both of her teenagers work as tutors for deprived children.

- For many parents, it's not necessary to be involved in the same type of community service that your teen does; it is enough to share the sense of giving and purpose. Indeed, it's best not to push your favorite causes. Let your teen find his own.

- Help your teen through the disappointment that can come with community service. Patricia was frustrated when she returned from a summer in South Dakota, where she took care of Native American children at a church-run daycare center. "It was a hard experience at the end of every day," she recalled sadly. "We would drop off the kids to their screaming, abusive mothers, in run-down houses, knowing that the kids didn't want to go back. I got very discouraged."

Fortunately, Patricia was able to talk to her mother about how she felt. The resolution was to continue her interests in Native American culture through a research project that uncovers Indian stereotyping in the media. "You have to be of a certain mind-set to deal with some of the upsetting community service," advises a school counselor. "But there are all kinds of places that need help."

The High School Years

As high school teens continue to form their individual identities and ideas, they worry less about what their friends do and think than they did during their middle-school years. Certainly, friendships are important, and there is still much peer influence over their choice of music or their way of dressing and speaking; but there is also a newfound recognition that they can hang out with whomever they please. This doesn't mean that the races comfortably mix in high school. Indeed, self-segregation and racial tension prevail now and through the college years. What has changed is that the older teen is able to evaluate what is happening and can choose what to do about it. When a Salvadoran twelfth grader describes the racial tension in his school, he observes: "We don't like discrimination, but it exists, and we participate a little bit. We have to learn love. In this country it is a challenge."

Aristotle described adolescence as a time of "strong passions." "They love too much and hate too much. They think they know everything and are sure about it," he said. Centuries later, that observation still holds, but parents must realize the value of those passions.

One of the reasons for the strong difference in opinion between teens and their parents is that older teens need to find, and then exercise, their independence. Invariably in the process of becoming her own person, a teen will blame adults for many of society's ills. Adolescence is a time of self-righteousness, a critical time when the child looks at the world, shakes her head and says, "What a mess you people have made. My generation and I can do much better."

This is also the age when morals and values are finally understood by the teen, not as impositions but as necessary ways to bring order and fairness to society. In this spirit, older teens often become deeply involved in social causes or community service that appeal to their particular concerns and interests.

Unfortunately, older adolescence is still a time of pitfalls. In addition to racism and violence, these young adults may stumble into monstrous and debilitating traps related to drug abuse, alcoholism, eating disorders, the spread of AIDS and teenage pregnancy. Complicating all this is the way teenagers are depicted in the entertainment media as selfish, aimless and immoral. It's not a pretty picture, and it rightfully worries parents, who often are close enough to their own teenage years, to make inevitable, though weak, comparisons. Parents should be wary of equating their child's adolescent experiences to memories of their own. This is not to say that parents shouldn't impress their values or beliefs upon their teenager. We hope that parents today believe that all human beings deserve a fair chance at a decent life, no matter what their race or economic circumstance. And we encourage them to strongly instill that belief in their teenagers. There lie our hopes for the twenty-first century.

35

Be Honest: Talk About Uncertainties

Ablack mother who is active in diversity programs at her child's school struggles with the negative reaction she has toward her older teenage son dating a white girl. "She's a nice girl, but she came to our house for dinner and used black slang; I'm not sure I liked that. I don't want to tell him, but I know what problems he's going to face in the future if he stays with her."

Parents may claim to embrace all peoples, but when faced with racial issues, particularly those that threaten their child's physical and emotional well-being, they can react with uncertainty, anger and even shame.

If and when something happens to stir up those old familiar feelings of racial prejudice, it's best to admit it. Let your teenager know how you honestly feel and don't try to sugarcoat your reaction. Kids know when you're faking it, and they are especially good at knowing when parents are trying to act like they aren't worried. By having an honest dialogue (be sure it's two-way), you are showing respect for your child and his experience, and you are gaining a better understanding of what your teen is going through and how he is coping. You are also more likely to come up with a solution than if you keep your concern to yourself.

Be aware if your uncertainties and prejudices are especially piqued when you read the newspaper or watch the news on television. Be honest with your child about how you feel towards such national and local issues as race-related violence or job inequalities. When a white parent admits to her teenager how she falls into the pattern of associating blacks with crime, she can do more than expose her prejudice—she can involve her teenager in the process of reevaluating and changing her way of thinking. The parent can say: "Help me understand how I got these feelings. Are they justifiable? If not, how can I change them?"

Share, but don't overload your child with any personal struggle you may have with prejudice. Bring it up, but don't harp on it to the point that it becomes a major issue between the two of you. If parents are totally focused on race to the exclusion of everything else, they can prompt a teenager to shut down communication and avoid the topic all together.

Give time and space for your child to absorb what you have said. Try not to demand his instant opinion or to overreact to his retorts. He may not respond right away because he, too, finds it hard to deal with and doesn't want to do the "work" that is involved. Or, he may react emotionally and dramatically at first and then come back later with a more thoughtful response. Keep in mind that it takes a great deal of sophistication on the part of the teen not to overreact to a parent's admission of prejudice.

A white mother of a fifteen-year-old recalled how she was torn between what she called her liberal beliefs and her concern that her son was developing more friendships with blacks than with whites. "I was both proud of him and worried about him," she explained to a group of mothers at a parent-school discussion on racism. Instead of admitting to her son that she had these conflicted feelings, she kept hedging, saying that she missed hearing about and not seeing some of his old friends. She didn't want to admit that her concern about this change in his social life was racially motivated, thinking it would be offensive to suggest that too many black friends is somehow bad or a problem. Finally, they had a "heated argument" where she had to face how she really felt. "Intellectually, I had always denied my prejudice, out of shame and guilt, because it went against my values," she told the group of mothers. "But he showed me that it was still there, and I realized then that I had to work on it. And I'm impressed by the fact that he knows what he's doing."

With a mixture of regret for her past and pride for her son's generation, she noted: "When I was growing up, my parents never discussed these things. Kids today are much more reflective, and parents can be much more involved and open."

36

Beware of Your Nonverbal Messages

A racially mixed group of high school students gathered in a classroom during their lunch hour to discuss how their parents talk about prejudice and race. Only a few of the twenty students recalled having in-depth conversations or debates about race with their parents. Despite this lack of communication, the majority of the students claimed to know how their parents felt about people of other races. "It's the subtle emotion," explained a sixteen-year-old white girl disdainfully. "You just know what they're thinking. Like the time I was watching the news and my mom walked in just as they were showing films of a package store getting robbed by a black man. She let out this disgusting gasp and left the room."

Nonverbal messages are as powerful as a written contract or an emotional speech. Recall a recent incident in which someone you know made you feel uncomfortable or angry or very happy. It may be difficult to describe what it was about the person that attracted or alienated you. It had to do with feelings or sensations you got from being in the person's presence, things communicated through body language and facial expression.

That same dynamic is a factor when we avoid talking to our children about race. Even if we make an effort to hide our feelings, our children, especially teens, hear us loud and clear.

Tune in to your nonverbal prejudice. What body language do you evidence when you're around someone of another race? What facial expressions do you use when your child is describing a problem in school that you sense must be racially based? Many whites are reluctant to talk about race because they say they don't know how to bring up the subject without exposing long-held prejudice; or they simply don't know what words to use. Ironically, their prejudice is blasting nonverbally at full decibel.

"Our lack of discourse is dividing the races," says a parent, "and that silence is on both sides." Whites say that they consider the silence or "sullen look" that blacks often direct toward them to be deep-seated anger or bitterness that can't be penetrated; on the other hand, blacks describe a silent nervousness and lack of eye contact on the part of whites as fear—and racism. A black father angrily explains: "If I'm walking down the street, the white guy crosses to the other side. When someone sees me in the parking lot, they lock their car door. And when I'm talking to a white clerk in a store, she talks over my head to someone else."

All of us should be more sensitive to our negative nonverbal communication. A closer examination may make us feel ashamed enough, or inspired enough, to speak out. Anything is better than withdrawing into our racist silence.

37

Speak Clearly and from the Heart

"May I tell you something?" the black teenage boy asked Barbara after she met with his class. "My parents told me there was one human race divided into ethnic groups, and they were put on this world all made in the same image, and that we all go through the same pain." He swung a chair around and sat down, then went on to say that he had seen serious racial problems at his high school, where the majority of students are black and the minorities are white and Hispanic. This teen said he uses his parents' advice to form his own philosophy for survival: "We separate ourselves from others who are actually very much like ourselves. That's why I don't even use the term *race* anymore."

If you want to get your teen's attention about race, it's best not to come up with lengthy, convoluted arguments or heavy, guilt-ridden sermons. Instead, try simple, brief messages spoken from the heart. In Barbara's interviews with teenagers, it was apparent that those with the strongest convictions were those whose parents expressed clearly their values and responsibilities toward all human beings. In addition, these messages were charged with energy that was deeply felt by the parents and treasured by the child, as if they were gifts.

Don't be afraid to call on emotion; if your message has verve and passion, it will be long remembered by your child and turned to when most needed. Barbara was not surprised to find that emotional expression was generally less forthcoming from white parents. From personal experience, she believes that this reticence of expression and lack of passion stem from the fact that whites haven't had the depth of pain and experience that minorities have had. Also, research shows that whites are culturally and traditionally more controlled in their expression of their beliefs—though there are always variations of communication within all cultures, depending on such factors as economics, education and family patterns of speaking. Whatever the reason, there is a lesson to be learned from the minority children who have preserved and honored their parent's counsel. Like the fifteen-year-old girl who cherishes the words her mother told her when she left Peru to live in the States and go to school: "If you want respect, you have to honor respect."

"She used those exact words five years ago," the girls says in a voice that breaks with the weight of the memory.

Take your belief and turn it into a challenge or a provocative question. Help your teen to think about these heartfelt issues by offering questions that encourage reflection or debate. For example, "What would your school and life be like if our system returned to segregation?" Or "Is class discrimination less offensive than race discrimination?"

"My father always challenged me by asking, 'How would you feel if you were discriminated against?'" says seventeen-year-old Anthony. The question is an especially good one for older teens who are searching for ways to improve society.

Offer simple directives that broaden your child's experience; bring him out of his small, self-focused world and into the bigger world around him. For example, telling your child to "put yourself in another's shoes" can produce thoughts that serve him well from nursery school into the older adolescent years, and the rest of his life.

Your teen is going to be receiving strong and conflicting messages from different parts of society—especially from the media and his peers. All the more reason for you to get in there with a powerful thought that carries him through the fray. White parents especially should take the plunge—and speak from the heart.

38

Challenge "Self-Segregation"

Lunch time at the local high school on a beautiful day means "get out and eat out"—nobody wants to stay in the dismal cafeteria. Groups of kids brown-bag it on the school's front lawn; other groups head for nearby fast-food restaurants. A visitor notes immediately that most of the kids gather according to their color: Hispanics with Hispanics, blacks with blacks, whites with whites. Just a few clusters are mixed: an Asian face with whites, several blacks with whites. This is integration at the close of the twentieth century.

Critical and privileged segments of our society often point to this evidence of "self-segregation" among high school and college students and say "See! Integration hasn't worked."

One would have to agree that integration *as we practice it* hasn't solved our problems—but that is because it has been poorly managed, not because it is wrong or inappropriate. Adolescence is a time for seeking and defining one's identity; it's also a time when avoiding criticism and fitting in with friends are crucial to one's self-esteem. It's little wonder then that kids hang around other kids like themselves; that's where they feel accepted and safe. Teens have always formed cliques according to class and neighborhoods or special interests, such as sports, music or the visual arts. Today, when kids choose to be with their own race, or their own shades of color, we needn't get too alarmed about it *unless* their choice of company is motivated by hatred and divisiveness within a larger group.

The word *segregation* usually describes a negative isolation; and now a part of society loudly proclaims "self-segregation" as the choice of minorities and a problem for everyone. But as one high school principal notes: "People don't care about how white kids hang out together, but they are quick to point the finger at how the blacks 'self-segregate.'" Perhaps a better word would be "separate." Parents should understand that there are times when teens as a group need to separate themselves from other groups in order to celebrate their identity.

A white mother asked her child, "What would prevent you from sitting down with the black girls in the lunch room?" She answered easily, "I have friends there, and I wouldn't want to intrude." The mother didn't interpret her daughter's view as racist, but rather as "reasonable." Unfortunately, she didn't encourage her daughter to give more of an explanation, such as why she thought her presence would have been intrusive; or, when she thought it would it be okay to join the group for lunch.

If teenagers feel physically threatened by another race or are afraid to mingle with others for fear of rejection by their own group, the roots of racism may have taken hold. Parents need to balance the tendency that teens have to separate themselves with tangible opportunities for their child to know and mingle with people of other races. That's the only way to defuse myths about people who are different. "When you get to know other people, they aren't so scary," says one young student.

A school vice-principal in the Midwest advises a group of parents during a meeting on prejudice: "Kids need opportunities to mix with others in a safe and creative setting, and we need to help them find it, because they aren't going to go looking on their own."

Most parents are not very likely to—and shouldn't—say to their teen, "Now let's find a place where the races meet and mix." Instead, the search starts with an interest. If your child loves to sing, you look for a chorus or a theater group; if she loves to play soccer, you look for a team that plays at her age level. When you look, make sure the activity is racially mixed. There are scores of opportunities for your child to have an integrated experience; in addition to extracurricular activities at school, they include: church and synagogue youth groups, where kids work together on community projects as well as educational, recreational and spiritual activities; local recreation departments that sponsor athletic teams; the YMCA and YWCA for classes, sports or special programs like "Horizons," where teenagers learn environmental skills such as rock climbing, cave exploring and teamwork in the wilderness; Boys and Girls Clubs; and camps and schools that teach drama, music or fine arts.

There's little doubt that teenagers from different races and backgrounds who work together on a mutual project are less likely to harbor racial prejudice. When a multiracial group of kids gathers to paint scenery for a school play, they joke and talk, all the while learning that they have similarities and differences that don't stand in the way of them getting to know one another. Because of their shared interest and goal, they are on equal ground and safe to discover one another's personalities and viewpoints.

When Barbara interviewed teenagers who had made interracial friendships in their extracurricular activities, they were relaxed about their situation. "We don't think about it; it's no big deal" was the usual response. "They're just my friends."

39

Face Your Teen's Prejudice

"**I** don't understand it," says a white mother whose son attends a public school marked by heavy racial discord. "I raised my child to be fair to everyone, and now that he's in high school, he's angry and prejudiced."

A black teacher shakes his head over the fact that today's kids are facing problems their parents never had to face: "Little wonder they react and think differently than their parents ever did." Another mother says regretfully, "I thought it was just a stage my daughter was going through, and I figured her prejudice would go away as she matured, but it got worse in college."

Most parents are unprepared if and when their teens develop outspoken prejudice against other races or against segments of their own race. Bewildered, some parents ignore the problem, or deep down, they may even side with their child's reaction. But all parents need to take their teens' prejudice and anger seriously in order to help them identify the source of the problem and to find a remedy.

First, get in touch with what is happening in your teen's life to cause this hatred and fear. Ask him to describe the circumstance in detail: Who or what group is threatening to him and how is it shown? One African American teen described to his parents how he is a victim of prejudice from his black friends who have ostracized him from their group because they claim he "dresses white." A biracial teen laments to her mother about her unwillingness to socialize with either all-white or all-black groups of friends: "It's really hard. I'm not comfortable with either group."

Once you know the facts, help your teen delve further into the reasons behind the prejudice on both sides. For example, if he says he hates and fears kids who racially harass him in the halls between classes, get him to see why they act the way they do. Explain that bullies have low self-esteem and often come from homes where they were routinely criticized and physically punished.

Most important, point out that he is making generalizations about an entire race based on one group of bullies—and that this is exactly the type of thinking that produces racism. Finally, help him understand that bullies exist in all races.

Offer positive examples of how race relations can work, using what you know from his school, your workplace and your neighborhood or among public figures. He may argue that his life is different, but stick to your point. He'll consider your examples well after your discussion.

Don't make his bad feelings about race put a heavy guilt trip on you. You may have done your best to raise him, but he has had plenty of outside influence from society.

Other tips in dealing with your child's prejudice: When you hear racist language, say so. A mother who raised her son in the inner city of Atlanta tells him, "It offends me when you use the word 'nigger.'" He retorts, "It's no big deal; it's like saying 'hell.'" "No, it's not," she insists. "It's like saying 'nigger,' and it's not right or allowed."

This same mother advises parents with prejudiced children that "when you have to work on the problem, do it alone with the child and not with other family around, so you don't embarrass him. Try not to raise your voice; if you do, he will, too. Say something to show how much you love him even during this time. For instance, 'I care about you; I know how you can care for others, so it hurts to hear you talk this way.'"

"I'm afraid my child is going to feel this way the rest of his life," said one concerned parent. He probably will if you don't keep making your convictions clear. And as long as you leave the door open for discussion, you've still got a chance for a better solution. By helping him figure out why people act the way they do, and by showing him that he is stereotyping an entire race through some bad experience, you help him fight prejudice.

40

Epilogue: Don't Give Up. Keep the Faith.

Will there ever be respect between the races? Will our country ever be rid of racism?

Challenge yourself about the future, about the demise of racism. Can it be a reality, or is it an impossible dream? Challenge your friends on the topic in private conversation or other parents in public dialogue, and most important, question and challenge your children. Their responses will keep the task of combating racism in the forefront, and spur you on to work even harder at knowing and understanding others. As one parent says: "I'm discouraged, but it doesn't mean that we shouldn't keep trying."

At the end of each interview, we asked whether there was any hope for the future. Though people's answers varied, there were very few who expressed no hope at all.

Of those who were hopeful, we asked why.

We found that blacks, Hispanics, Asians and Native Americans consistently gave the same response: "We have no other choice." Few whites gave this answer, perhaps for several reasons: They don't think about the consequences of racism as much because they're on top, in control; also, they don't have a history of race-based oppression. Many whites choose to look the other way—after all, it's not their problem; it's the minorities, especially the blacks, who are screaming. The reality is, however, that if things continue the way they are, and the minority populations continue to grow, it's not only racial relations in our country that will get worse for whites; everything will—economically and socially. "What we do need to consider," says the white father of three teens, "is that if we don't do something to change and improve the present-day situation among the races, it will be even worse for our children and their children. So we have to choose hope for the children's sake."

We asked: "When do you think the racial climate is going to change for the better? Will our children see the change, or will it take another generation?"

"It's not going to change, not in my lifetime, not in my kids' lifetime," a black father said adamantly at the end of the interview, which included six parents from a private school. The Latina and white mothers in the room didn't agree. The Latina mother even said, "It's going to happen, and happen fast."

Her answer was rare. Even the most optimistic agreed that if it happens, it will come slowly. "It will continue and spread," insisted a black mother in Chicago, "but it will take years."

Unquestionably, many Americans are frustrated with the slow progress toward ending prejudice. But many whites claimed that the slow rate of change is proof that racism will eventually be extinguished. Often, they gave the example of how when they were young, their parents would be appalled if they dated anyone of another race, or even of another ethnic group within their own race; and now as parents, they "see no problem" with the fact that their children are in mixed-race marriages.

We asked: "How do you maintain a sense of hope?"

Through faith or spirituality was the answer for a large majority, no matter what their race.

"Through the community" was the next answer most often given. Over and over, we heard people of all races insist that the battle against racism cannot be won solely by parent and child, or by family unit; for it to truly take hold, they said, it has to be a community effort. "When people band together and say they just won't stand for things going the way they are going," says a school counselor in Washington, D.C., "that's when things change. It takes a community to get action."

This is not to say that our individual efforts to be role models for our children are secondary. Indeed, you can't have a community effort without all individuals being committed. Fairness and understanding are first taught by word and example, by parent to child. In Lawrence, Kansas, a black mother of two young children ended a public discussion on racism by encouraging parents of all races to see themselves as powerful role models. She held her one-month-old baby as she spoke, making her words especially inspiring.

"I think that change is going to take place because, individually, we touch so many people in our lives. As long as we maintain our principles and our self-integrity and keep a sense of spirituality, we're going to impact a lot of people around us, and that eventually will make a difference, especially with our children."

Bibliography

Churchill, Ward. *Indians Are Us?: Culture and Genocide in Native North America.* Monroe, ME: Common Courage Press, 1994.

Comer, James P., M.D., and Alvin F. Poussaint, M.D. *Raising Black Children.* New York: Penguin, 1992.

Derman-Sparks, Louise, and the A.B.C. Task Force. *Anti-Bias Curriculum: Tools for Empowering Young Children.* Washington: National Association for the Education of Young Children, 1989.

Dickerson, Bette J. *African American Single Mothers: Understanding Their Lives and Families.* Thousand Oaks, CA: Sage Publications, 1995.

Du Bois, W. E. B. *Black Reconstruction in America, 1860–1880.* 1935. Reprint. With an Introduction by David Levering Lewis. New York: Atheneum, 1992.

Elkind, David. *Parenting Your Teenager.* New York: Ballantine Books, 1993.

Genovese, Eugene D. *Roll, Jordan, Roll: The World the Slaves Made.* New York: Vintage Books, 1974.

Gibbs, Jewelle Taylor, ed. *Young, Black and Male in America: An Endangered Species.* Westport, CT: Auburn House, 1988.

Ginott, Haim G. *Between Parent and Teenager.* New York: Avon Books, 1971.

Greenspan, Stanley I. *Playground Politics: Understanding the Emotional Life of Your School-Age Child.* New York: Addison-Wesley, 1993.

Hale, Janice E. *Unbank the Fire: Visions for the Education of African American Children.* Baltimore: Johns Hopkins University Press, 1994.

———. [Janice E. Hale-Benson] *Black Children: Their Roots, Culture, and Learning Styles.* Baltimore: Johns Hopkins University Press, 1986.

Holmes, Robyn M. *How Young Children Perceive Race.* Thousand Oaks, CA: Sage Publications, 1995.

Hopson, Darlene Powell and Derek S. Hopson. *Different and Wonderful: Raising Black Children in a Race-Conscious Society.* New York: Fireside, 1992.

———, with Thomas Clavin. *Raising the Rainbow Generation.* New York: Fireside, 1993.

Kunjufu, Jawanza. *Countering the Conspiracy to Destroy Black Boys.* Chicago: African American Images, 1985.

———. *Countering the Conspiracy to Destroy Black Boys.* Vol. 4. Chicago: African American Images, 1995.

———. *Hip-Hop vs. MAAT: A Psycho/Social Analysis of Values.* Chicago: African American Images, 1993.

Ponterotto, Joseph G., and Paul B. Pedersen. *Preventing Prejudice: A Guide for Counselors and Educators.* Newbury Park, CA: Sage Publications, 1993.

Reddy, Maureen T. *Crossing the Color Line: Race, Parenting and Culture.* New Brunswick, NJ: Rutgers University Press, 1994.

Riley, Patricia, ed. *Growing Up Native American.* New York: Avon Books, 1993.

Steinberg, Laurence, and Ann Levine. *You and Your Adolescent.* New York: HarperPerennial, 1991.

Warren, Rita M. *Caring: Supporting Children's Growth.* Washington: National Association for the Education of Young Children, 1994.

Weatherford, Jack. *Indian Givers: How the Indians of the Americas Transformed the World.* New York: Fawcett Columbine, 1988.

Index

About the Authors

BARBARA MATHIAS grew up in Milwaukee in a family of seven children in which she was third in line and the oldest girl. Her father was in advertising and her mother eventually went on to be a newspaper reporter. Like her mother, Mathias didn't begin her writing career until well into motherhood—when the youngest of her five children was a toddler and her oldest was a young teenager.

For the next ten years Mathias wrote between carpools and from her home just outside Washington, D.C. Her award-winning articles on family, women and relationships appeared in numerous publications, including *The Washington Post*'s "Style Plus" page and *Family Circle* magazine. In the late 1980s she got out of the house and was the People/Health editor for the *Journal Newspapers* serving Maryland and Virginia. In 1989 she worked in public affairs at the Brookings Institute where she introduced the idea of offering lunch hour seminars on family life.

Mathias left Brookings to freelance for *The Washington Post* and research the elusive topic of biological sisterhood. Her subsequent book, *Between Sisters: Secret Rivals, Intimate Friends* (Delta), broke the ground in the 90s for reconsidering one's siblings. Mathias has been on major network television and radio talk shows. Recently divorced, she often feels she is switching roles with her adult children, who keep close tabs on her new-found freedom.

MARY ANN FRENCH is the single, working mother of a six-year-old boy. They live in the heart of Washington, D.C., not far from the neighborhood where Mary Ann was raised in a boisterous home with four brothers, three sisters and energetic parents. Her mother is an early-childhood development specialist; her father is a surgeon and public health physician who moved the family to Africa for ten years while he established and ran a project that strengthened health delivery systems in twenty countries.

Currently a staff writer for *The Washington Post*'s Style section, French brings her perspective to Americana that's both obvious and obscure, antebellum and postmodern, hiphop and bebop. She traveled with the Marines to Somalia to write about Operation Hope, and to South Africa to cover aspects of that country's first democratic elections.

On these shores, she reported the 1988 presidential elections for the *Baltimore Sun*'s Washington bureau, primarily following Jesse Jackson. Also from Washington, she covered Congress and wrote a Sunday op-ed column for the *St. Petersburg* (Fla.) *Times*. She covered the artificial heart experiment for the *Louisville Courier-Journal*, and she has written for a number of national magazines.

Before settling in as a writer, French crewed on boats in the Caribbean and helped launch women's agricultural coops in West Africa. She has a master's degree from the Johns Hopkins School of Advanced International Studies.